P9-BBU-902

*Totally
Tasteless*

Totally Tasteless

THE COLLECTED WORKS (SO FAR) OF BLANCHE KNOTT

BALLANTINE BOOKS   NEW YORK   1983

Library of Congress Catalogue Card Number: 83-91907

The jokes in this book originally appeared in *Truly Tasteless Jokes* and *Truly Tasteless Jokes Two*.

Selected jokes from *What Do Wasps Say After Sex?* by Matt Freedman and Paul Hoffman, Copyright © 1981 by Matt Freedman and Paul Hoffman. Published by St. Martin's Press.

ISBN 0-345-31400-X
Manufactured in the United States of America
First Edition: November 1983

To Don, who knows quality when he sees it.

Contents

Totally
Tasteless

Ethnic Jokes— Variegated

Why do Italian men have mustaches?
So they can look like their mothers.

❧

What's Irish and comes out in the springtime?
Patio furniture.
(Paddy O'Furniture . . . get it?)

❧

Did you hear about the advertisement for Italian army rifles?
"Never been shot and only dropped once."

What do you get when you cross a Pole and a Chicano?

A kid who spray-paints his name on chain-link fences.

⤳

What are the first three words a Puerto Rican child learns?

"Attention K-Mart shoppers . . ."

⤳

Two guys are walking along, and Harry keeps going on about how he hates Italians. "Greasy wops," he grumbles, "always makin' noise. And talk about *dumb*. . . . Wish they'd go back where they came from."

In the middle of this harangue, they come to a street corner where there's an organ grinder. He really looks the part: one earring, tattered gypsy jacket, and is loudly singing "O Sole Mio." So Phil is astonished when Harry digs a $1 bill out of his pocket and gives it to the organ grinder's little monkey.

"What'd you do that for?" he asks. "I thought you *hated* Italians."

"I do," sighs Harry, "but they're so cute when they're young."

Why do Puerto Ricans throw away their garbage in clear plastic bags?

So Italians can go window shopping.

∽

A black, an Irishman, and an Italian are trying out for a TV quiz show. The emcee explains that all they have to do is complete the sentence and spell the word they come up with. All three candidates nod in understanding. The announcer's voice booms out the first question: "Old MacDonald had a—"

Farm," says the Italian. "F...a...r...m...e."

"I'm sorry," says the announcer. "Right word, wrong spelling. Next, please: Old MacDonald had a —"

"House," says the Irishman. "H...o...u...s...e."

"So sorry," says the announcer. "Wrong word, right spelling. Next, please: Old MacDonald had a—"

"Farm!" says the black. "E...i...e...i...o."

∽

Why did God invent golf?

So that white people could dress up like black people.

A Jew and an Irishman are having a lofty discussion about sex, the Irishman maintaining that it's work and the Jew that it's pleasure. Unable to come to an agreement, they agree to discuss it further at another date.

At their next meeting, the Irishman announces triumphantly that he had checked with his priest. "He says it's work purely for the purpose of procreation, you see?"

The Jew is far from satisfied, and goes to talk the matter over with his rabbi. Reporting on his findings to the Irishman, the Jew says, "My rabbi says it must be pleasure, because if it was work we'd have the blacks do it."

❧

What's the difference between an Italian grandmother and an elephant?

Fifty pounds and a black dress.

❧

What do you call a Mexican with a vasectomy?

A dry Martinez.

❧

How do you solve the Puerto Rican problem?

Tell the blacks they taste like fried chicken.

What do you get when you cross a Chinaman and a hooker?

Someone who'll suck your laundry.

⁓

A four-passenger plane is halfway across the Pacific when it becomes obvious that it's having serious engine troubles. Eventually the captain comes over the PA system to make a grave announcement. "Passengers," he says grimly, "I'm afraid that with our current load, this plane is never going to make it to land. In fact, the only way any of us are going to make it, since there's no cargo aboard, is by jettisoning passengers. Now since I'm the captain, I've got to stay put, but I'm sure we've got three gentlemen aboard who will sacrifice themselves for the greater good."

"*Vive la France!*" exclaims a young Frenchman and, clutching his beret, opens the emergency hatch and plummets out of sight.

After a slight pause, a stout British man stands up. "Long live the Queen!" he says proudly, making for the door.

There is a long pause, following which a big Texan stands up. Grabbing the hapless Mexican sitting next to him, he tosses him out of the hatch, shouting, "Remember the Alamo!"

During a strategic battle of World War II, a Jew, a black, and an Irishman had the misfortune to be blown to smithereens by the same shell. And so they found themselves at the gates of heaven, where St. Peter greeted the Irishman first. "My boy," he said, "it's obvious to me that you've been fighting on the side of Good and Justice, and to reward you, I'm giving you a second chance at life on earth. Get along now."

Rather unable to believe his good fortune, the Irishman stumbled into the bivouac to report to his commanding officer. "My God, man," stammered the incredulous officer, "how'd you get back here . . . and what happened to your companions?"

"Well, sir" explained the soldier, "St. Peter let me back to earth for free, and when I left the Jew was trying to get St. Pete down from $100 to $19.99, and the black was trying to get someone to co-sign a loan."

On a transatlantic run a freighter came across three survivors of a shipwreck, bobbing about, sunburned and thirsty, in a rubber raft. The freighter's captain, a Britisher, leaned over the side and shouted, "I'd like to rescue you fellows, but I've a few questions first." Of the first man, a hard Welshman, he asked, "What was the worst disaster in naval history?"

"That would be the sinking of the *Titanic*," replied the Welshman, and the captain threw down a rope and pulled him up.

The next question he posed to the Irishman: "Can you tell me how many died?"

"I'd say about 1250 people," came the reply, and a rope was dropped over the side to pull him aboard.

"You're from Australia, aren't you?" said the captain to the lone man in the raft, turning away from the rail. "Name 'em."

∼

How do they say "fuck you" in Los Angeles?
"Trust me."

∼

What's black and white and red all over?
An interracial couple in an automobile accident.

∼

Did you hear that Alitalia and El Al were merging to form a new airline?
It's going to be called Well I'll Tell Ya . . .

This little Jewish guy, couldn't weigh more than seventy pounds, goes to Houston on business. He checks into the hotel, which is fifty stories high, and is shown into a suite the size of a ballroom. Overwhelmed, he goes down to the bar and is served a glass it takes him both hands to lift. "Everything's big in Texas, pal," says the bartender with a wink.

When his steak dinner arrives, the plate can't even be seen. "Hey, everything's big in Texas," says the waiter.

Finally, overcome by all of this, the little guy decides it's time to hit his super-king-size bed, only to lose his way in the hotel's vast corridors. Opening the door of a darkened room, he falls into the swimming pool with a great splash—and surfaces to shriek, "Don't flush!"

∽

Did you hear about the Italian engineer who invented a car so energy-efficient it didn't need any gas at all?
It's called the Ronzoni Downhill.

∽

Or about the Italian driver in the Indianapolis 500 who had to make seven pit stops . . . to ask directions?

How do you get forty Haitians in a shoebox?
>   Tell 'em it floats.

∽

What's an innuendo?
>   An Italian suppository.

∽

Why do Mexicans drive low-riders?
>   So they can cruise and pick lettuce at the same time.

∽

What did the Mexican do with his first 50-cent piece?
>   Married her.

∽

Why don't Mexicans have barbecues?
>   The beans fall through the grill.

∽

How many cigars does it take to kill ten Mexicans?
>   Juan Corona.

In America, they say, "It's 10:00—do you know where your children are?"

In England, they say, "It's 10:00—do you know where your wife is?"

In France, they say, "It's 10:00—do you know where your husband is?"

In Poland, they say, "It's 10:00—do you know what time it is?"

∽

Why don't Puerto Ricans like blow jobs?
    They're afraid they'll interfere with their unemployment benefits.

∽

What's the difference between an Italian mother and a Jewish mother?
    The Italian mother says, "If you don't eat all the food on this plate, I'll kill you."
    The Jewish mother says, "If you don't eat all the food on this plate, I'll kill myself."

∽

What's brown and has holes in it?
    Swiss shit.

What do they use in a Mexcan baptism?
    Bean dip.

～

Why do Mexicans eat refried beans?
    Ever seen a Mexican that didn't fuck things up
    the first time around?

～

Why is Italy shaped like a boot?
    Because they couldn't fit all that shit into a
    sneaker.

～

How does God make Puerto Ricans?
    By sandblasting blacks.

～

Did you hear about the Italian who picked his nose
apart to see what made it run?

What's Jewish foreplay?

    A trip to the jewelry store followed by a half hour of begging.

Puerto Rican foreplay?

    "Is your husband back from work yet, Carmen?"

Irish foreplay?

    "Brace yourself, Bridget!"

WASP foreplay?

    Drying the dishes.

Black foreplay?

    "Don't scream or I'll kill you."

Did you hear about the Greek boy who left home because he didn't like the way he was being reared?

    He came back because he couldn't leave his brothers behind.

Why do Mexican women wear long skirts?

    To hide the no-pest strips.

Why do Italians bury their dead with their asses sticking up out of the ground?

    So they'll have somewhere to park their bicycles.

Know what Greek lipstick is?
  Preparation H.

~

What's the definition of a cad?
  An Italian who doesn't tell his wife he's sterile until she's pregnant.

~

How come the Mexican Army only used 600 soldiers at the Alamo?
  They only had two cars.

~

How do you kill an Italian?
  Smash the toilet seat down on his head while he's getting a drink.

~

Why do Mexicans' cars have such small steering wheels?
  So they can drive with handcuffs on.

What's the definition of a maniac?
    An Italian in a whorehouse with a credit card.

∾

How do you get two Mexicans off your roof?
    Jerk one off and the other'll come too.

∾

How many people from New Jersey does it take to change a light bulb?
    Three: one to do it, one to watch, and the third to shoot the witness.

∾

What do you call a Vietnamese family with one dog?
    Vegetarians.
What do you call a Vietnamese family with two dogs?
    Ranchers.

∾

How many Mexicans does it take to grease a car?
    One, if you hit 'em right.

Why didn't the black man want to marry a Mexican? He didn't want the kids to grow up too lazy to steal.

❦

Do you know about the world's shortest books?
Polish Wit and Wisdom
Jewish Business Ethics
Italian War Heroes
and *Negroes I Have Met While Yachting*

❦

How can you tell there's an Irishman present at a cock-fight?
He enters a duck.
How can you tell a Pole is present?
He bets on the duck.
How can you tell an Italian is present?
The duck wins.

❦

"Help! Help!" cried the young woman as she staggered up the steps of the police station. "An Irishman molested me."

"How'd you know he was Irish?" inquired the sergeant at the desk.

"I had to help him," she gasped.

"Dad," said the kid, "can I have five dollars to buy a guinea pig?"

"Here's ten dollars, son. Go find yourself a nice Irish girl."

෴

Did you hear about the man who was half Polish and half Italian?

He made himself an offer he couldn't understand.

෴

A Jew, a Hindu, and an Irishman were traveling together, and as night fell they came to a little country inn. The innkeeper explained apologetically that only two beds were available in the inn but that he would be glad to make up a comfortable cot for the third man in the barn. So the three travelers drew straws, and it fell upon the Jew to sleep in the barn.

In a few minutes there was a knock on the door, to which the innkeeper responded. "I'm so sorry," explained the Jew, "but there is a pig in the barn, and my religion forbids me to sleep under the same roof as a pig."

The Hindu had taken the next straw, and out he went. In a few minutes, though, there was another knock, and the innkeeper opened the door on the Indian fellow. Apologizing gracefully, he explained that his religious persuasion forbade him to share shelter with a cow, and there was indeed such a creature in the barn.

Finally, out went the Irishman. In a few minutes there was yet another knock on the door, which the innkeeper answered. On the sill stood the pig and the cow.

❧

An Italian, a Pole, and a black man moved out to California to seek their fortunes. The Italian and the black got jobs right away, but weeks went by without the Pole finding employment. Finally, one evening he announced to his roommates that he had a big interview the next morning at nine and, setting the alarm well ahead of time, he went to bed.

In the middle of the night the other two snuck into his room, smeared his face and hands with blackface, and set the alarm forward. When it went off in the morning, the Pole leaped from his bed, pulled on his clothes, and dashed off so as not to be late for the critical interview.

The interviewer invited him in with an apologetic expression on his face. "I'm sorry to have brought you here for nothing," he said, "but I'm afraid we simply don't employ blacks."

"Blacks! What are you talking about?" sputtered the Pole. "My name is Joe Bukarski!"

"I'm so sorry, Mister Bukarski, but we simply don't make any exceptions in our hiring policy."

"But I'm not black!"

"I'm sorry you're taking it so hard. You may not think you're black, but have you looked in a mirror lately?"

The Pole got up and went over to a mirror near the door. Staring in disbelief at his undeniably black reflection, he stammered, "Oh my God—they woke the wrong guy!"

❧

The Italian and the Polish parachutists were arguing about who was best at folding a parachute. Unable to resolve their dispute on the ground, they decided to go up in the plane and judge by the mid-air performance of their chutes. The Pole jumped first, pulled the cord, and started floating toward the earth. The Italian jumped, pulled the cord—and nothing happened. He pulled the safety cord—nothing. In a matter of seconds he whizzed past the Pole, plummeting like a stone.

"Oh," shouted the Pole, yanking off his harness, "so ya wanna *race!*"

❧

A Jew and a Chinaman were in a bar together. The Jew brought up the subject of Pearl Harbor, reprimanding the Chinaman for the disgraceful role his countrymen had played. He protested vehemently, pointing out that the raid had been made by the Japanese, and that China was in no way to blame.

"Japanese, Chinese, they're all the same to me," retorted the Jew.

Pretty soon the Chinese fellow started talking about the tragic sinking of the *Titanic*, asking the guy if he didn't feel some degree of personal responsibility about it.

"Hey, wait a minute!" protested the guy. "The Jews didn't have anything to do with the sinking of the *Titanic*—it was sunk by an iceberg!"

"Iceberg, Goldberg," said the Chinaman, "they're all the same to me."

ᕦᕤ

What's eight miles long and has an IQ of forty?
   The St. Patrick's Day Parade.

ᕦᕤ

A widower was devoted to his only daughter and naturally was concerned when she decided not only to get married but to marry a Greek. Blushing furiously, he sat her down to discuss the facts of life, but she brushed him off, assuring him she knew all about those things and not to worry.

"Well, just one thing," the father implored. "If he asks you to turn over, you don't have to."

The young couple got married and were extremely happy until about six months had gone by. Embracing his wife in bed, the Greek said, "Why don't you roll over, dearest?"

"Oh, no, you don't!" she said. "My father said if I don't want to, I don't have to."

"Whatsamatter," he said, "don't you wanna get pregnant?"

༄

Sammy Davis, Jr. stepped onto a bus in Jacksonville, and the bus driver said, "Nigger, get to the back of the bus."

"But I'm Jewish," protested Davis.

"Get off."

༄

An Italian, a Jew, and a Greek were walking down the sidewalk when—ZAP—a bolt of lightning came down and killed all three instantly. Up they went to the gates of heaven, where St. Peter greeted them warmly.

"Saint Peter, you can't do this to us," they protested vehemently. "We're young men in the prime of life. *Please* let us go on living."

St. Peter pondered the issue. "Well," he finally pronounced, "I'll let you go back to Earth on one condition: that from this moment on, you all promise to abstain from your one most favorite activity."

The young men lost no time in giving their fervent promises, and—WHAM—found themselves back walking down the sidewalk. What should they come across on the corner but a pizza parlor. The Italian broke into a sweat. Unable to resist temptation, he dashed in, ordered a slice, took a bite, and—POOF!—vanished in a puff of smoke. The Jew and Greek were understandably sobered by this event and continued walking, when a quarter rolled across the sidewalk.

His eyes lighting up, the Jew bent over to pick it up.

And the Greek disappeared.

❧

What do you call a fat Chinaman?
    A chunk.

❧

What do you get when you cross a Mexican and an Iranian?
    Oil of Olé.

❧

Did you hear about the football game between Italy and Poland? The Italians all started arguing about who was going to be quarterback and walked off the field, and three plays later the Poles won.

A Pole, an Italian, and an Irishman have planned an expedition across the Sahara, and at the appointed time each shows up with the baggage critical to his survival.

Motioning to his flask, the Irishman says, "It's going to be a thirsty business, this crossing the desert, and I'll need a drop to drink."

Nodding his approval, the Italian points out his potful of pasta. "Itsa gonna be hungry work," he says.

They look across at the Pole, who is carrying nothing but a turquoise-and-white left front door to a '57 Chevy. "It's going to be plenty hot out there," he explains, "and I want to be able to roll down the window."

༄

A Pole, an Italian and a Jew are marooned on an island. While walking along the beach, one of them comes across an old bottle. He rubs it and out comes a genie, who is empowered to grant them each their dearest wish.

"Ah," says the Italian, "let me go back to the Old Country, where the wine is sweet and the women are beautiful." Poof!—he vanishes.

"For me," says the Jew, "I want to go to the Holy Land and live out the rest of my days with my people." Poof!—he vanishes.

"Gee," says the Pole, "it's kind of lonely here. I wish I had my friends back."

What's six miles long and goes four miles per hour?
A Mexican funeral with only one set of jumper cables.

∾

Why did God give Mexicans noses?
So they'd have something to pick in the off season.

∾

The English teacher in a public school in Spanish Harlem decided it was time for the weekly vocabulary lesson. "What's the difference between select and choose, Ramon?" she asked.

"Select is when you pick something," he answered, "and choose are what Puerto Ricans wear on their feet."

∾

An Irishman, a Frenchman, and a Pole walk into a bar.
The Irishman orders a WW.
"What's a WW?" asks the bartender.
"A whisky and water," he explains.
The Frenchman orders next, and politely requests an RW.

"What's *that?*"

"A red wine," he explains.

The Pole thinks a bit, and finally leans across the bar to ask for a fifteen.

"What the hell is that?" asks the beleaguered bartender.

"A seven and seven," answers the Pole.

❧

Did you hear about the Italian who emigrated to Poland?

He raised the IQ of both countries.

❧

What are the three occasions on which an Italian man visits his priest?

His first communion. When he gets married. Before his electrocution.

❧

What do you get when you cross a Puerto Rican and a Chinaman?

A car thief who can't drive.

How do you fit forty-seven Puerto Ricans in a Volkswagen?

Use a blender.

How do you get them out?

Doritos.

∿

"Did you hear they sent up a Japanese astronaut?"

"No, first I've heard of it."

"Well, I heard them say on the radio that there's a little nip in the air."

∿

How do you keep an Englishman happy in his old age?

Tell him a joke when he's young.

∿

When the Irishwoman answered her front door it was only to hear the sorry tidings, shouted through the crack of the open door, that her husband had been killed. "And that's not the worst of it, I'm afraid, Ma'am," said the foreman. "He was run over by a steamroller."

"I'm in my bathrobe," said the new widow. "Could you slip him under the door?"

A Pole, an Italian, and a Puerto Rican jump off the Empire State Building. Who lands first?

Answer #1: The Italian, because the Puerto Rican stops to write on the walls, and the Pole stops to ask directions.

Answer #2: Who cares?

❧

Why are there no Puerto Rican doctors?

Because you can't write prescriptions with spray paint.

❧

What does NAACP stand for?

Negroes Are Actually Colored Polacks.

❧

How many people does it take to bury a Puerto Rican?

Five. One to lower the Puerto Rican, and four to lower the radio.

❧

What do you call three Irishmen sitting on the lawn?

Fertilizer.

How many people does it take to bury an Italian?
Two. There're only two handles on a garbage can.

❧

What do you call a Puerto Rican midget?
A speck.

❧

What do you get when you cross a Jew and a Puerto Rican?
A superintendent who thinks he owns the building.

❧

Two Poles and a black worked for a construction company and got into the habit of working together —until the day the black fell off a scaffold eleven stories high. When the police got to the scene, there wasn't too much left of the fellow, so the officer in charge turned to the two distraught Poles. "Listen, guys," asked the cop, "was there anything distinctive about this man?"

"No, he was just a regular guy," sniffed one of the Poles.

"Hey wait a minute!" piped up the other. "He had two assholes!"

"Are you bullshitting me?" asked the cop. "How the hell would you know?"

"Because every time we went into the bar around the corner for a beer at the end of the day," said the Pole happily, "the bartender would say, 'Here comes that stupid nigger with the two assholes!' "

∽

What do you get when you cross a Mexican and an octopus?

Got me, but it sure can pick lettuce.

∽

A Pole and a Jew were in a bar watching TV when the late-night news came on. The first sensational story was of a berserk woman poised on a window ledge seven stories up.

"I'll bet you a hundred dollars she won't jump," said the Pole to the Jew.

"You got a deal," said the Jew, sticking his hand out a few moments later when the woman plunged to a gory death. The Pole sadly forked over the money and ordered another drink, only to look up in astonishment as the other fellow tugged on his sleeve and tried to hand the hundred dollars back.

"It's all yours," he protested. "You won the bet fair and square."

"Nah," said the Jew, "I saw it all happen on the six o'clock news."

"I saw it happen on the six o'clock news, too," said the Pole, "and I never thought she'd do it *again* at eleven."

❧

A Jew, a Pole, and a black man all died on the same day and went to heaven, where they were warmly greeted by St. Peter. "Good to see you guys," said St. Peter. "One quick quiz and I'll be able to formally admit you to heaven."

"Just a sec," said the Jew. "Being a Jew, I've had it rough all my life, and I'd like to know if I can expect any religious persecution in heaven."

"Certainly not," said St. Peter. "Spell *God*."

"Well, now," said the Pole, "being Polish, I've been treated like shit, and I'd like to make sure I'm not going to encounter any more of that sort of stuff."

"No way," said St. Peter. "Spell *God*."

"Saint Peter," said the third man, "as you can see, I'm black, and I've had to endure a lot of prejudice in my life. Can I expect any more of that in heaven?"

"Of course not," said St. Peter. "Spell *chrysanthemum*."

Black

What's the definition of worthless?
    A seven-foot-two-inch black with a small cock who can't play basketball.

∾

Did you hear the Harlem High School cheer?
    Barbecue, watermelon,
      Cadillac car;
    We're not as dumb
    As you think we is!

There was this football coach who wasn't too pleased with the way his team was performing; their record was 0–6 and it was already half way through the season. He didn't know quite what to do about it, though, since he couldn't figure out whether the play book was too complicated or whether the players were simply unable to play any better. Finally he decided that the best solution was to simplify the play book, reducing the number of plays to something even the most thick-headed guy on the team could understand.

So after a particularly depressing defeat, he called his muddy and battered team together and explained that from now on they would only have to master four plays, and that he had simplified the calls as follows: NRR, NRL, SPDN, and WBK.

"What's dat agin, coach?" asked the quarterback, scratching his head.

"NRR," explained the coach, "stands for Nigger Run Right."

"NRL." he went on, "means Nigger Run Left, and SPDN means Same Play, Different Nigger. As for WBK, well that's White Boy Kick."

∾

What's tattooed on the inside of every negro's lip?
    Inflate to 50 psi.

Why do blacks wear high-heeled shoes?
　　So their knuckles don't scrape the ground.

❧

Why do blacks wear wide-brimmed hats?
　　So pigeons don't shit on their lips.

❧

Two black garbagemen in Atlanta were going about their rounds and came to the end of their route with the garbage truck absolutely full—and with one bag of garbage still sitting on the sidewalk. Being conscientious workers, they were reluctant to leave it, but the truck would not hold another ounce.

"Tell you what, Joe," said Sam. "You drive real slowly, and I'll hang on to the back of the truck holding that last bag with my body. We ain't got too far to go."

That was fine with Joe, and so he drove the truck off with Sam clinging, spread-eagled, to the back of the truck.

They rounded the corner and passed by two Southern gentlemen, who looked at the back end of the truck with considerable surprise. "Can you believe your eyes?" asked his companion. "They're throwing away a perfectly good nigger!"

What do you call a black millionaire physicist?
A nigger.

～

What do you get when you cross a black and a groundhog?
Six more weeks of basketball season.

～

How do you know Adam and Eve weren't black?
Ever tried to take a rib from a black man?

～

There was a black couple that already had eight fine children, and finally the wife implored her husband to have a vasectomy. After much cajoling, he made an appointment, and the morning of the operation his wife was astonished to see him leave the house dressed in white tie and tails and head for a big black limousine waiting at the curb. Responding to her quizzical look, he explained, "Honey, if you gonna *be* impo'tant, you gotta *act* impo'tant!"

A con man came into a small-town saloon, sidled up to the bar, and told the bartender he'd bet him $50 he could have him in tears in three minutes. "You got a deal!" said the bartender. "I haven't cried since I broke my ankle when I was ten."

So two and a half minutes went by in silence, and finally the bartender said, "You know, you only have thirty seconds left and I'm nowhere near tears."

"No problem," said the con man. "My friend Boo will be along any moment, and he'll have you bawling in no time."

"Boo who?" asked the bartender . . . and then sheepishly handed over the fifty bucks.

The con man proceeded down the bar to where a black guy was nursing a beer, and made him the same offer. "Man, ah ain' cried since ah was a baby," said the black guy. "You on!"

A minute, two minutes ticked by, and the black guy spoke up, pointing out that time was running short. "Don't you worry," said the con man, "my friend Boo is due right about now and you're going to weep."

"Who be Boo?" asked the black guy.

＄

Did you hear about the little black kid who got diarrhea?

He thought he was melting.

What do they call a woman in the Army?
    A WAC.
What do they call a black woman in the Army?
    A WACcoon.

∾

Why do blacks always have sex on their minds?
    Because of the pubic hair on their heads.

∾

A crowd gathered on a Harlem sidewalk where a white guy was jumping up and down on a manhole cover energetically, shouting, "Twenty-eight! Twenty-eight!" Finally one big black guy was unable to restrain his curiosity. "What you doin' dat fo'?" he roughly questioned the jumper.

"Listen, it really makes you feel great. You wouldn't believe how it relieves tension, cools you out. . . . Why don't you try it for yourself?"

So, somewhat suspiciously, the big black guy started jumping up and down on the manhole cover. Just as he was getting into a rhythm, the white guy pulled the cover out from underneath him, and the black tumbled down the hole.

Cheerfully replacing the cover, the guy started jumping up and down again, shouting, "Twenty-nine! Twenty-nine!"

Did you hear about the African sex researcher?
  Kunte Kinsey.

⌇

Did you hear about the new Black French restaurant?
  Chez What?

⌇

What do you call four blacks in a '57 Chevy?
  A blood vessel.

⌇

What are three French words all blacks know?
  Coupe de ville.

⌇

What's black and shines in the dark?
  Oakland.

⌇

Why did God create the orgasm?
  So blacks would know when to stop screwing.

What did Lincoln say after his five-day drunk?
"I freed *who?*"

~

Why do blacks wear white gloves?
So they don't bite off the end's of their fingers
when they're eating Tootsie Rolls.

~

It was the first day of the new term at Princeton,
and a black freshman was learning his way around
the campus. Stopping a distinguished-looking upper-
classman, he inquired, "Say, can you tell me where
the library is at?"

"My good fellow," came the reply, "at Princeton
we do not end our sentences with a preposition."

"All right," said the freshman, "can you tell me
where the library is at, asshole?"

~

Three people die at the same moment and arrive at
the gates of heaven at the same time. St. Peter greets
them warmly and asks the first, "And what did you
die of, may I ask?"

"The Big H," says the fellow, a florid, overweight
type.

"Ah yes," nods St. Peter, "the number one killer of men your age. Please step this way."

The second person, a withered old man, attributes his death to "the Big C."

"So sorry to hear it," murmurs St. Peter. "This way, please." And to the next person in line he asks, "Cause of death?"

The big black woman says, "De big G."

"What in heavens name is 'the Big G'?"

"Dat's gonorrhea," she answers.

"Madam," says St. Peter stiffly, "one does not die of gonorrhea."

"You does if you gives it to Big Leroy."

❧

This black guy walks into a bar with a beautiful parrot on his shoulder.

"Wow!" says the bartender. "That is really something. Where'd you get it?"

"Africa," says the parrot.

❧

What has six legs and goes "Ho-de-do, ho-de-do, ho-de-do?"

Three blacks running for the elevator.

What's another word for cocoon?
N-nigger.

∾

What's black and white and goes rolling along the boardwalk?
A black and a pigeon fighting over a chicken wing.

∾

How do you shoot a black man?
Aim for the radio.

∾

What do you call a black boy with a bicycle?
Thief!

∾

What's the new Webster's definition of the word "confusion?"
Father's Day in Harlem.

What's the new Webster's definition of the word "reneg?"

Shift change at the carwash.

❧

A black guy knew he had it made when the old brass bottle he found in the back yard turned out to have a genie in it. Any three wishes he had would be granted, the genie informed him.

"I wanna be rich," said the black man. The back yard filled up with chests of gold coins and jewels in the blinking of an eye.

"I'm no fool," said the black. "I wanna be white." And there he stood, white, blond-haired, and blue-eyed.

"Thirdly, I never want to work another day in my life."

And he was black again.

❧

A successful black banker got into the latest fad: hang gliding. He went out and bought a beautiful, sky-blue jumpsuit, took his hang glider, and proceeded to float off over the woods.

Two old white farmers, Royce and J.T., had picked the same day to do a little hunting. Royce looked up and said to J.T., "Shit! Dat's de biggest goddam bird I ever seen!"

"Let's get 'em," said J.T.

They fired off several rounds, but the glider floated serenely over the trees and out of sight.

"Hell, Royce," said J.T., "I b'lieve we dusted dat bird."

"Shit, I *know* we dusted 'em," said Royce. "Did you see how fast it dropped dat nigger?"

What do you get when you bury a thousand blacks up to their necks?

Afroturf.

An old Southern planter goes into the hospital and is informed by the doctor that his condition is pretty serious. In fact, he's going to require a heart transplant.

"Well, doctor," drawls the planter, "you'd best get on with it. But whatever you do, just don't give me the heart of a nigger."

When he comes out of the anesthetic, the doctor is leaning over his bedside anxiously. "Cal," he says, "I got some good news and some bad news. I *had* to use a nigger's heart."

Cal pales.

"But the good news is: Your dick is three inches longer.

What do you call a black millionaire industrialist?
A tycoon.

~

What do you call a black Frenchman?
Jacques Custodian.

~

What do you call a black test-tube baby?
Janitor in a Drum.

~

Do you know why so many blacks were killed in Vietnam?
Because every time the sergeant said "Get down," they stood up and started dancing.

~

Why are the palms of black people's hands white?
Because they were all leaned up against cop cars when God spray-painted.

Did you hear about the new perfume for black women?

It's called Eau-de-doo-dah-day.

❧

How do you keep little black kids from jumping up and down on the bed?

Put Velcro on the ceiling.

How do you get 'em down?

Invite some Mexican kids over and tell them it's a piñata party.

❧

What color's a black who's run over by a steamroller?

Flat black.

Jewish

*I*f *Tarzan and Jane were Jewish, what would Chee-*
tah be?

A fur coat.

～

What do you get when you cross a JAP and an
Apple?

A computer that never goes down.

～

The Jewish grandmother was terribly proud of her
four-month-old grandson, so she took him with her
down to Miami Beach. The first morning she got him

all decked out, and down they went to the beach, where she set him by the shore to play. But no sooner had she sat down in her beach chair than a huge tidal wave rose up and swept the baby away.

"God," she said, standing up and shaking her fist at the sky, "you aren't very nice! Here was this little baby boy, whose mother carried him for nine months, barely around for four. We haven't even had time to get to know him or give him a happy life."

In another instant the wave returned, setting the infant down unharmed on the sand. The grandmother looked him over, looked right back at the sky, and snapped, "He had a hat!"

∿

Did you hear about the new brand of tires—Firestein?
They not only stop on a dime, they pick it up.

∿

What's the difference between a JAP and a bowl of Jell-O?
Jell-O shakes when you eat it.

There was a seventy-year-old *mohel* (that's the person who performs ritual circumcisions for Jews, in case you didn't know) who found to his horror that his hands were beginning to shake. Needless to say, in his line of work that was a serious liability, and he dashed off to see if he could get some sort of insurance policy.

A week later the insurance agent called him up. "Listen," he said, "I've got some good news and some bad news."

"Let me have it," said the *mohel.*

"Well the good news is that I can get you a million-dollar policy, for one hundred dollars a year, no problem," said the agent.

Wiping his forehead in relief, the *mohel* asked, "So what's the bad news?"

"There's a two-inch deductible."

❧

What's a JAP's favorite position?
    Facing Bloomingdale's.

❧

What's the difference between a JAP and the Bermuda Triangle?
    The Bermuda Triangle swallows semen.

How do you know when a JAP's having an orgasm?
She drops her emery board.

⌒

Why do JAPs only sleep with circumcised men?
They want 20% off *everything*.

⌒

Did you hear about the new movie called *Altered Suits* ?
It's the story of a Jewish man who takes acid and buys retail.

⌒

What's the worst thing for a JAP about having a colostomy?
Trying to find shoes to match the bag.

What did one mink say to the other as they were taken out of their cages to be killed and skinned?
"See you in Temple."

∽

You can imagine the excitement when a Martian spaceship landed in a sunny suburban field and proved to be filled with intelligent, amicable beings. Jane Pauley managed to be the first television personality on the scene, and the chief Martian agreed to an exclusive interview on the "Today" show the next morning. As the cameras started to roll, she told the Martian how curious people on Earth were about his people, so she thought she'd just ask him a few general questions. The Martian graciously said that was fine with him.

"Tell me," said Pauley, nervously clearing her throat, "do all of your people have seven fingers and toes?"

"Yes," said the Martian, waving his slender green appendages in the air.

"And two heads? Everyone has those?"

"Oh yes," said the Martian, nodding both enthusiastically.

"And also those lovely diamonds and rubies embedded in their chests as you do?" asked Pauley.

"Certainly not," snapped the Martian. "Only the Jews."

What's the difference between a Jewish mother and a vulture?

A vulture waits till you're dead to eat your heart out.

∾

What's a JAP's idea of natural childbirth?

Absolutely no makeup.

∾

Three nice Jewish widows decided to take an exotic vacation together, so off they went to darkest Africa on a photographic safari. The expedition pitched their tents deep in the jungle and the next morning set out on their first excursion, but Naomi was too tired to go along, despite her companions' dismay. And no sooner were they out of earshot than a huge gorilla swept down from a tree, grabbed Naomi, and dragged her off to his nest to screw her mercilessly for three days. That night, Sophie and Zelda, hysterical with grief, found a battered and bloody Naomi, semiconscious, outside their tent. Naomi was immediately airlifted back to Mount Sinai Hospital in New York where her two friends hovered by her side until, after many days, she was able to speak.

"Naomi, darling, speak to us," beseeched her friends. "Did that creature abuse you? Are you in pain? What's wrong? Say something!"

"What should I say? He never calls," sobbed Naomi, "he never writes . . ."

What's the difference between circumcision and crucifixion?

In a crucifixion, they throw out the whole Jew.

❧

The devout Jew was beside himself because his son had been dating a *shiksa*, so he went to visit his rabbi. The rabbi listened solemnly to his problem, took his hand, and said, "Pray to God."

So the Jew went to the synagogue, bowed his head, and prayed, "God, please help me. My son, my favorite son, he's going to marry a *shiksa*, he sees nothing but goyim..."

"Your son," boomed down this voice from the heavens, "you think *you* got problems. What about *my* son?"

❧

What's a JAP's dream house?

Fourteen rooms in Scarsdale, no kitchen, no bedroom.

God is cleaning house, and he comes across these Commandments taking up valuable closet space. So he goes down to earth and offers them to the Roman emperors. "Not interested; we're too busy having orgies," is the response. Next God tries the Pharaohs, but the answer comes back, "Sorry, too busy building pyramids." Finally giving up, God takes a walk in the desert, where who should He run across but Moses. "Would you be interested in some nice Commandments by any chance?" God asks.

"How much?" asks Moses.

"Why, they're free."

"I'll take ten."

❧

Why do JAPs have crow's-feet?
From squinting and saying, "Suck *what* ?"

❧

Why do JAPs close their eyes while they're fucking?
So they can pretend they're shopping.

❧

What's the difference between a JAP and a canoe?
Canoes tip.

What did Mr. Mink give Mrs. Mink for Christmas?
    A full-length Jew.

∾

It's quiz time in the parochial school, and Brother Michael offers a fifty cent prize to the student who can name the greatest man who ever lived.

"Columbus," offers Joey Rizzo.

"Pope John Paul II," volunteers Jan Milowski.

"St. Francis of Assisi," says Irving Feldman, whispering to a classmate, "I would've said Moses, but business is business."

∾

What's a JAP's favorite wine? (Say it aloud and it sounds like "whine.")
    "I wanna go to Floooorida . . ."

∾

What's the difference between a JAP and a barracuda?
    Nail polish.

What does a JAP do during a nuclear holocaust?
  Gets out her sun reflector.

～

Do you know how to keep Jews out of the country club?
  Let one in, and he'll keep the rest out.

～

This black guy was walking down 125th Street, kicking rubbish out of his way, when he spotted something amid the trash that gleamed strangely. It turned out to be an oddly shaped bottle, and when he rubbed it, a Jewish genie appeared. "I'll give you two wishes," intoned the genie.

"Far out," said the black guy. "First, I want to be white, uptight, and out of sight. Second, I want to be surrounded by warm, sweet pussy."

So the genie turned him into a tampon.

The moral of the story: You can't get anything from a Jew without strings attached.

～

Why is money green?
  Because the Jews pick it before it's ripe.

Why did the Jews wander in the desert for forty years?
  Somebody dropped a quarter.

∾

Why do Jews have such big noses?
  Because air is free.

∾

What happens when a Jew with an erection walks into a wall?
  He breaks his nose.

∾

What's a Jewish dilemma?
  Free ham.

∾

What's the definition of a queer Jew?
  Someone who likes girls more than money.

How do you stop a Jewish girl from fucking you?
Marry her.

෴

Did you hear about the bum who walked up to the Jewish mother on the street and said, "Lady, I haven't eaten in three days."
"Force yourself," she replied.

෴

Why do JAPs use gold diaphragms?
Their husbands like coming into money.

෴

What's the difference between karate and judo?
Karate is a method of self-defense, and judo is what bagels are made of.

෴

What's the difference between a JAP and poverty?
Poverty sucks.

How did they know Jesus was Jewish?
> Because he lived at home until he was thirty, he went into his father's business, his mother thought he was God—and he thought his mother was a virgin.

∾

How do you tickle a JAP?
> Gucci, Gucci, goo.

∾

How many JAPS does it take to change a light bulb?
> Two. One to call Daddy, and one to get out the Diet Pepsi.

∾

What do JAPs make for dinner?
> Reservations.

∾

How does a JAP eat a banana? (This is a visual joke, so pay attention.)
> Pretend you are holding a banana in your right hand. With left hand, peel off the three or four

strips of peel about halfway down the banana. Continuing to hold peeled banana in right hand, place left hand behind head. Force head down over banana.

⌒

Why do JAPs wear bikinis?
 To separate the meat from the fish.

⌒

What do you get when you cross a JAP and a hooker?
 Someone who sucks credit cards.

⌒

How many Jewish mothers does it take to change a light bulb?
 "None, dahling, I'll sit in the dark . . ."

⌒

Did you hear that the limbo was invented by the Jews?
 Yeah, from sneaking into pay toilets.

A Palestinian gentleman was taking a walk on the West Bank when he was brutally beaten by a gang of young Israeli toughs. Deciding to take matters into his own hands, he bought a huge German Shepherd trained to kill on command and went out to seek revenge.

It didn't take him long to see the perfect victim: a little old Jewish man walking a little dog that somewhat resembled a dachshund. The Palestinian loosed his ferocious dog—but to his astonishment he saw the little dog pin his dog to the ground and swallow his dog whole, all within thirty seconds.

"What kind of dog *is* that?" he gasped, ashen-faced.

"Well, before we had his nose fixed he used to be an alligator," explained the little Jewish man.

Polish

Did you hear about the Pole who heard on the radio that 90 percent of all accidents happen within a 10-mile radius of the home?

He moved.

~

How about the Polish abortion clinic?
There's a year-long waiting list.

~

One night the Pope is saying his bedtime prayers when God Himself comes down from heaven to listen to them. Then, sitting on the Pope's bed, He says,

"Listen, you've been such a good Pope and devoted follower that I'm going to grant you any wish you'd like."

The Pope is overcome with emotion, and for a little while he can't think of anything to say, but then he confesses to one thing that really gets to him. "As you know, God," he says, "I'm very attached to my country of origin. And one thing that really irritates me sometimes is all those stupid Polish jokes."

"No problem," says God magnanimously. "From this moment on, there shall be no more Polish jokes." Smiling, He says, "Listen, I have to be getting back to heaven, but before I take off, is there anything else I can do?"

The Pope thinks and thinks, finally coming out with it. "M&M's," he pronounces.

"M&M's?" says God. "Gee, I've always thought they were harmless enough, melting in your mouth and all that . . . but I'll be glad to abolish them if it really means a lot to you."

"Well you see," says the Pope, "I'm not getting any younger, and it's getting harder and harder to peel them."

∾

Did you hear how the Polish hockey team drowned?
Spring training.

Blanche Knott

Know how you can tell when a firing squad is Polish?
    It stands in a circle.

⌇

How do you break a Pole's finger?
    Hit him in the nose.

⌇

Hear about the lazy Pole?
    He married a pregnant woman.

⌇

What's the smallest room in the world?
    The Polish Hall of Fame.

⌇

Hear about the Pole who went out and brought four
new snow tires?
    They melted on the way home.

Or the Pole who lost $50 on the football game?

$25 on the game and $25 on the instant replay.

❧

Then there was the Pole who had the asshole transplant.

The asshole rejected him.

❧

How about the Polish girl who wanted to trade her menstrual cycle for a Honda?

❧

These two Poles go for a drive in the country, and when nature calls, they stop at an outhouse in a field. One fellow goes in first, and when ten minutes go by and he's still in there, his friend walks over and says, "Stan, are you all right?" Opening the door, he sees Stan poking around in the hole with a big stick. Stan explains that he managed to drop his overcoat down the hole.

"Listen," says his friend, "forget about the coat, okay?"

"Yeah, sure," says Stan. "It's not the coat I want, it's the sandwich in the pocket."

Then there was the Polish girl who said she'd do anything for a fur coat, and now she can't button it over her belly.

∼

Why do Polish stadiums have Astroturf?
To keep the cheerleaders from grazing.

∼

This Polish guy ordered a pizza with everything on it. When it came out of the oven, the guy asked him if he'd like it cut into four or eight pieces. "Make it four," said the Pole. "I'll never be able to eat eight."

∼

What's green and flies over Poland?
Peter Panski.

∼

Did you hear about the Pole who had body odor on one side only?
He didn't know where to buy Left Guard.

What about the Polish woman who thought Moby Dick was a venereal disease?

～

Two Poles walk into the post office and the first thing that catches their eye is a bunch of "Wanted" posters, in particular a shot of a mean-looking black guy beneath a banner that says "Wanted for Rape."

"You know," said one Pole to his friend, "they get all the good jobs."

～

A Pole has a big date, so he goes to the drugstore to buy some condoms. "That'll be $2.59 plus tax," says the clerk.

"What?" exclaims the Pole. "They don't stay up by themselves?"

～

Two Polish girls were walking down the street on a Saturday afternoon. One looks over and notices that her friend is walking a bit oddly, with her legs far apart. "Zelda," she asks, "why are you walking like that? Is something wrong?"

"Hey, I got a big date tonight," says Zelda. "My hair's in curlers."

Why are there no ice cubes in Poland?
They lost the recipe.

❧

Did you hear about the Pole who keeps a store of empty beer bottles handy . . . for his friends who don't drink.

❧

What do Poles say before picking their noses?
Grace.

❧

Joe Kowalski emigrates from Poland to America, filled with excitement at the promise his new land holds. He gets into a taxi at the airport and instructs the driver to take him to the Yimca Hotel. Perplexed, the cabbie goes over to another driver, who explains that his passenger means the YMCA. "He must be Polish—that's where they always want to go."

Joe is astonished when the cabbie asks him if he's Polish. How did he know? he wonders. He makes a vow to learn perfect English and become expert in the ways of his new country so that never again will he be taken for a foreigner, let alone a Pole. So he studies and studies, and finally decides it's time to give his English a field test. Repeating the phrase over and over to get it letter-perfect, he goes out to the corner store. Standing at the counter, he says in perfect English, "May I please have a quart of milk, a dozen eggs, and a quarter pound of Swiss cheese?"

"You Polish or something?" asks the proprietor.

"Why, yes, but . . . how did you know?" stammers Joe. "Did I not say it right?"

"You said it fine," says the fellow behind the counter, "but this is a hardware store."

❧

Why don't Polish women breast-feed their babies?
   It hurts too much when they boil the nipples.

❧

Why do Polish men make lousy lovers?
   Because they always wait for the swelling to go down.

❧

What's this? (Puff out your cheeks.)
   A Polish sperm bank.

What do you call a Pole with 1500 girl friends?
    A shepherd.

∽

Why are there no Polish ballerinas?
    Because when they do splits, they stick to the floor.

∽

Why are "Polish" and "polish" spelled the same way?
    Because Webster didn't know shit from Shinola.

∽

What happens when a Pole doesn't pay his garbage bill?
    They don't deliver anymore.

∽

Did you hear about the Pole who won a gold medal in the Olympic Games?
    He had it bronzed.

There's this farmer with a two-seater outhouse, and one morning he happens to be sharing it with a Pole. "Dammit!" says the farmer, pulling his pants up. "I dropped a quarter in there."

"Don't worry, I'll get it for you," offers the Pole, who gets up and proceeds to pull out a five-dollar bill and throw it down the farmer's hole.

"What did you do that for?" asks the bewildered farmer.

"Hell," says the Pole, "you didn't think I'd go down there just for a quarter, did you?"

❧

Did you hear about the Polish parachute?

It opens on impact.

❧

This Pole got married, but he was too dumb to know what to do on his wedding night.

"For God's sake, Stan," said his bride, "you take that thing you play with and you put it where I pee."

So he got up and threw his bowling ball in the sink.

❧

Did you hear that the Polish government bought a thousand septic tanks?

As soon as they learn to drive them, they're going to invade Russia.

Did you hear about the new Polish drink?
 Perrier and club soda.

❧

Why does the Pole always take a dime along on his dates?
 So that if he can't come, he can call.

❧

Why were the Poles pushing their house down the road in the middle of the winter?
 They were trying to jump-start the furnace.

❧

A Pole suspected his wife of infidelity and began to follow her movements. Sure enough, his suspicions were justified. Coming home from work early, he burst into the bedroom, catching his wife and lover in the act, and, crazed with grief, he put the pistol to his own head.
 "Don't laugh!" he shouted when his wife burst out in giggles. "You're next!"

❧

"Knock, knock."
 "Who's there?"
 "Polish burglar."

A group of scientists discovered an apelike creature in the wilds which they were certain was the Missing Link. The proof of their theory, though, required that a human mate with the ape in order to see what characteristics the progeny would take on. So they put an ad in the paper: $5000 to Mate with Ape."

The next morning a Pole called up in response to the ad and said he'd be willing to be part of the experiment. "But," he said, "I have three conditions."

The scientists agreed to hear him out.

"First: My wife must never know.

"Second: The children must be raised as Catholics.

"Third: If I can pay in installments, I'm definitely interested."

∽

Ever seen the Polish sex manual?

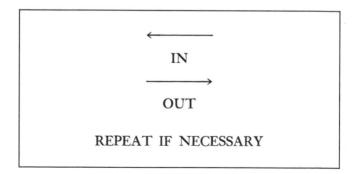

Why did the Pole spend all night outside the whore-house?

He was waiting for the red light to turn green.

∿

Lick cover of a book of matches, then bend it back so matches are exposed. Stick to forehead.
Ask, "What am I?"

A Polish miner.

∿

Did you hear about the Polish starlet?

She went to Hollywood and fucked the writer.

∿

The manager of a prosperous whorehouse in Warsaw one night found, to his dismay, that he was short of girls for the evening's entertainment. Thinking quickly, he dashed out and bought several inflatable fuck dolls, figuring that, given his average clientele, no one would know the difference. Soon he ushered a customer into a room that housed one of the new lovelies, assuring him he was in for an especially good time.

When the customer came out of the room a little

while later, the manager was waiting eagerly in the hallway. He winked at the fellow and asked, "Well? How'd you like her?"

"I don't know what happened," said the customer, shaking his head. "I bit her on the tit, she farted, and flew out the window."

༈

A stranger walks into a bar and announces to the barman, "Hey, fella! Have I got some terrific Polish jokes for you guys."

The bartender leans over to him and says, "Listen, if I were you I'd watch your tongue. The two 250-pound bouncers are Polish, I'm Polish and I ain't no midget, and every man in here is Polish."

"Oh, that's okay," said the stranger cheerfully. I'll talk v-e-r-y s-l-o-w-l-y."

༈

Do you know why the suicide rate in Poland is so low?

Because you can't jump out of a basement window.

༈

How can you tell a Polish Peeping Tom?
(Pull out front of own pants and look down.)

Why do Polish people have such beautiful noses?
They're handpicked.

❧

Did you hear about the two Polish hunters?
They were driving along when they came up to
a sign that said "Bear Left," so they went home.

❧

Or the Polish hunters who got themselves all set
up for a weekend of hunting? They gathered their
guns and the dogs and the ammunition and the orange
hats and tromped about for hours, but with no luck
whatsoever. And when they came out of the woods
at dusk, they looked around at all the other hunters,
who were carrying braces of pheasant and quail, ducks
and geese, even a deer or two.

"Gee," said one Pole to his companion, "everyone
else seems to be doing pretty well for themselves.
Whaddaya think we could be doing wrong?"

"I dunno," said the other. "Maybe we're not throwing the dogs high enough."

❧

What do you call a pretty girl in Poland?
A tourist.

Two Polish guys went away on their annual hunting expedition, and by accident one was shot by the other. His worried companion got him out of the deep woods, into the car, and off to the nearest hospital.

"Well, Doc," he inquired anxiously, "is he going to make it?"

"It's tough," said the doctor. "He'd have a better chance if you hadn't gutted him first."

A realtor is showing a new property to an affluent young couple, who are somewhat bewildered by his behavior. On every landing, the realtor stops to open the window and shout, "Green side up!" Finally, they ask why.

"I've got a Pole laying the sod," he explains, "and I've got to make sure he does it right."

Did you hear about the guy who made a million dollars in Poland with Cheerios?

He sold them as doughnut seeds.

Did you hear about the Polish car pool?

They all meet at work.

How come Poles don't go elephant hunting?
　　They get too tired carrying the decoys.

❧

How come Poles don't become pharmacists?
　　They can't fit the little bottles in the typewriter.

❧

How do you know when your house has been burgled by a Pole?
　　The garbage's been eaten and the dog is pregnant.

❧

Did you hear about the Polish bank?
　　You bring in a toaster and they give you ten thousand dollars.

❧

　　A young Polish girl was hitchhiking along the Interstate, and a big semi pulled over to pick her up. The driver was a serious CB addict, and the dashboard boasted an enormous CB radio.

"That's the best radio ever made," he explained to the bug-eyed girl. "You can talk anywhere in the *world* with it."

"No kidding," she gasped. "Boy, I would really love to talk to my mother in Poland."

"Oh, yeah?"

"I would give anything to talk to my mother in Poland."

"*Anything?*" he asked.

"Anything," she assured him.

"Well, maybe we can work something out," he leered, pulling his cock, by this time erect, out of his pants.

So the girl leaned over, bent down, and said loudly, "HELLO, MOM?"

❧

What are the three most difficult years for a Pole?
Second grade.

❧

Did you hear about the Pole who had a penis transplant?
His hand rejected it.

Two Poles are out fishing for the day, and they have a hell of a time: fish grabbing the hooks as fast as they can get them into the water. Finally, with the boat as full of fish as possible, they decide it's time to head for shore.

"But listen," says Stan, "why don't we mark the spot?"

"No problem," says Jerzy, who dives in and paints a big black X on the bottom of the boat.

Stan beams with pleasure, and they're almost back to the dock when his face wrinkles in consternation. "On, no!" he cries to Jerzy, "What if we don't get the same boat?"

∿

What's this?

A Polish coke spoon.

What does a Polish girl do after she sucks cock?
Spits out the feathers.

∽

What do Poles wear to weddings?
Formal bowling shirts.

∽

Did you hear about the Pole who locked his family in the car?
He had to get a coathanger to get them out.

∽

A Pole walks into his local bar and goes straight up to the bartender, who turns away in disgust at the handful of horseshit the Pole is holding.

"Hey, Harry," says the Pole, "look what I almost stepped in."

A young Polish guy wanted more than anything to become a cop, and went through the rigorous entrance exam, the last question of which was "Who killed Christ?" The would-be rookie went home excitedly and said to his wife, "Honey, I think they're putting me on a murder case!"

WASP

*W*hat's the definition of a WASP?
Someone who gets out of the shower to pee.

∾

How many WASPs does it take to change a light bulb?
Two. One to mix the martinis, and one to call the electrician.

∾

What do WASPs say after they make love?
"Thank you very much; it'll never happen again."

How can you tell the bride at a WASP wedding?
She's the one kissing the golden retriever.

∽

Where do WASPs eat?
Restaurants.

∽

What does a WASP do when his car breaks down?
Fixes it.

∽

How many WASPs does it take to change a light bulb?
One.

∽

Two WASPs were walking down the street. One turned to the other and said, "You know, you're my best friend but you never ask how I'm doing, how things are going, how's business?"

"Okay," said his friend, "how's business?"

"Fine."

What do WASPs do instead of making love?
    Rule the country.

∾

What does a WASP mom make for dinner?
    A crisp salad, a hearty soup, a lovely entree, and a delicious dessert.

∾

What do you call a WASP who doesn't work for his father, isn't a lawyer, and believes in social causes?
    A failure.

∾

How can you tell the only WASP in a sauna?
    He's the one with the *Wall Street Journal* on his lap.

∾

What's a WASP's idea of a welfare check?
    An Irish tartan.

Why did God create WASPs?
    Somebody had to buy retail.

∽

How do WASPs wean their young?
    By firing the maid.

∽

What's a WASP's idea of open-mindedness?
    Dating a Canadian.

∽

What do you get when you cross a Jew and a WASP?
    A pushy Pilgrim.

∽

What do you get when you cross a WASP and an Orangutan?
    I don't know, but whatever it is, it won't let you in *its* cage.

What do you get when you cross a WASP and a Puerto Rican?

Assault and battery.

∾

How can you tell a male WASP is sexually excited?

By the stiff upper lip.

∾

How many WASPs does it take to plan a trip to Israel?

Two. One to ask where, and one to ask why.

∾

What do little girl WASPs want to be when they grow up?

"The very best person I possibly can."

∾

Why did the WASP cross the road?

To get to the middle.

How can you tell the WASPs in a Chinese restaurant?
They're the ones not sharing the food.

∾

What's a WASP's idea of post-coital depression?
Not being able to reach *The New Yorker* from bed.

∾

How does a WASP propose marriage?
He asks, "How would you like to be buried with my people?"

∾

Two WASPs were making love when the man looked down and said, "Did I hurt you?"
"No," she replied. "Why?"
"You moved."

Helen Keller

How did Helen Keller burn her fingers?
Reading the waffle iron.

∿

How did Helen Keller's mother punish her?
By rearranging the living-room furniture.

∿

How did Helen Keller meet her husband?
It was a blind date.

Why were Helen Keller's fingers purple?
    She heard it through the grapevine.

∽

What did Helen Keller do when she fell down the well?
    She screamed her hands off.

∽

Did you hear about the Helen Keller doll?
    Wind it up and it walks into walls.

∽

Why does Helen Keller masturbate with one hand?
    So she can moan with the other.

∽

Why did Helen Keller's dog jump off a cliff?
    You would too if your name was Uggggrrrgggh.

Why was Helen Keller's leg yellow?
  Her dog was blind, too.

༄

How did Helen Keller go crazy?
  Trying to read a stucco wall.

༄

How did Helen Keller burn her ear?
  Answering the iron.

༄

What did Helen Keller's parents do to punish her for swearing?
  Washed her hands with soap.

༄

Did you hear about Helen Keller's new book?
  Around the Block in Eighty Days

How does Helen Keller drive?
    With one hand on the wheel and one hand on the
    road.

∾

What's Helen Keller's favorite color?
    Corduroy.

Handicapped

W hat do you call a guy with no arms or legs in the swimming pool?
    Bob.
What do you call the same guy in the ocean?
    Skip.
What do you call the same guy at your door?
    Matt.
What do you call the same guy tacked up on your wall?
    Art.

∽

Desperate about the state of her social life, a young woman resorted to the Personals Ads in the back of her local paper. In the ad she made it quite clear that what she was advertising for was an expert lover; she already had plenty of sensitive friends and meaningful relationships and what she now wanted was to get laid, to put it bluntly.

Phone calls started coming in, with each caller testifying to his sexual prowess, but none quite struck the young woman's fancy. Until one night her doorbell rang. Opening the door, she found a man with no arms or legs. "I'm terribly sorry," she stammered, "but my ad was quite explicit. I'm really looking for something of a sexual expert, and you . . . uh . . . don't have all the . . ."

"Listen," the man interrupted her, "I rang the doorbell, didn't I?"

∽

What's the hardest thing about eating vegetables?
   The wheelchairs.

∽

What's the definition of endless love?
   Ray Charles and Helen Keller playing tennis.

∽

Why do farts smell?
   So deaf people can appreciate them too.

How do you tell the blind guy in a nudist colony?
  It's not hard.

❧

There's this really shy guy who never leaves his room. Although he's desperately lonely for any sort of companionship, he's terribly self-conscious about the fact that he has a wooden eye, and even though it's not very noticeable he doesn't want to expose himself to ridicule. Finally his best friend says, "Look, if you ever want to do anything with your life you've simply got to get out and about. Come with me to the prom on Saturday."

With the greatest reluctance he agrees, and Saturday night finds him sitting on the bleachers in the high school gym while his friend dances away, until he notices a woman on the other side of the room. She's not beautiful—in fact she has a harelip—and he screws up his courage to approach her.

"Would you like to dance?" he asks.

Her face lighting up, she cries, "Would I? Would I?"

"Harelip! Harelip!" he shouts back.

❧

What has 30,000 feet and still can't walk?
  Jerry's kids.

This guy has a blind date, and when she comes to the door his worst fears are realized: she's a paraplegic. But he takes her out to dinner and the movies anyway, being a nice guy, and in the movie theater it doesn't take long for things to work up to the heavy-breathing stage. Still, there she is in her wheelchair, and he's pretty perplexed about how to take things to the next stage . . . if there's going to *be* a next stage.

"Don't worry," she whispers in his ear. "Take me to the playground, and I'll hang from the jungle gym."

So he does just that, and they manage to have a pretty good time. She gets a little dirty and scratched up in the process though, and he's somewhat apprehensive when her father comes to the door to let her in.

"You see, sir . . ." he begins, but her father interrupts him with effusive thanks. "Don't worry about a thing, young man. The last three guys left her hanging there."

⁓

Did you hear the one about the queer deaf mute?
    Neither did he.

⁓

What goes, "Marc! Marc!"?
    A dog with a harelip.

What goes, "Nort! Nort!"?
    A bull with a cleft palate.

∽

What's the New Jersey state vegetable?
    Karen Anne Quinlan.

∽

The mongoloid husband comes home from work and sits down at the kitchen table, hungry for dinner. Soon enough, his mongoloid wife puts down in front of him a plate with a piece of meat on it, nothing else.

"Where's the vegetables?" he asks.

"Oh, replies his wife, "they're not home from school yet."

∽

Bumper sticker: Hire the handicapped—They're fun to watch.

Totally Tasteless

Graffiti:

MUTANTS FOR NUKES

How do you get a one-armed Pole out of a tree?
Wave at him.

The nervous father-to-be was pacing outside the delivery room when finally the doctor emerged. "Oh, doctor!" he cried. "Is it a boy or a girl?"

"I'm afraid I have a bit of bad news," said the doctor gravely. "I'm sorry to have to tell you that your child was not born complete."

The father's face fell, but he said, "Well, I'm sure it can have a happy and complete life in any case."

"That's not all," said the doctor. "I'm afraid your child has no arms or legs."

"Oh," said the father. "At least I understand they're doing wonderful things with braces and prostheses these days."

"It's not going to be easy," said the doctor. "You see, your child was born with no torso. In fact, your child is only a giant ear."

The father sighed and said, "Well, I'm sure my wife and I can make the best of it."

The doctor said, "I'm afraid that's not the worst of it. It's deaf."

༄

What do you get when you cross a mongoloid with a one-legged Pole?

A Polaroid One-Step!

༄

Bob was an avid golfer and, even at seventy-two, could still hit a fine drive. But finally he went in to his doctor to complain that his eyesight was getting so bad that he often couldn't see the ball.

"Well, Bob," said the doctor, "you know, when you get older something's got to go, and there's not much I can do about it. Now, I do have this patient named Joe—he's getting on in years and not as sharp as he used to be and he's deaf as a post, but he's got twenty-twenty eyesight. Why don't you take him with you the next time you go golfing?"

The arrangement seemed a little curious to Bob, but worth a try, and so the next Saturday he found himself out on the fairway with Joe and hit a beautiful drive.

"Well, Joe," he said, turning to the old guy, "did you see it?"

"Oh, yes," said Joe, "clear as day. If only I could remember where it landed."

❧

Who was the meanest man in the world?

The guy who raped the deaf-and-dumb girl, then cut off her fingers so she couldn't yell for help.

❧

Little Herbie had been blind since birth. One day at bedtime, his mother told him that the next day was a very special one. If he prayed extra hard, he'd be able to see when he woke up in the next morning.

The next morning she came into Herbie's room to make sure he'd prayed hard the night before. "Well then, open your eyes and you'll know that your prayers have been answered."

Little Herbie opened his eyes, only to cry out, "Mother! Mother! I still can't see!"

"I know, dear," said his mother. "April Fool."

Nine months to the day following their wedding, the Coopers had a baby. Unfortunately, it was born without arms or legs—without even a torso. It was just a head. Still, the Coopers loved and cared for their child, spoiling and indulging it. Finally after twenty years, they took a much-needed vacation, and whom should they meet on the cruise ship but a European doctor who had recently achieved a medical breakthrough. "I know," he said, "how to attach arms and legs to your child, how to make him whole."

The Coopers cut their trip short, rushed home and into the room where the head lay in its crib, and said, "Honey, Mom and Dad have the most wonderful surprise for you!"

"No," shrieked the head, "Not another hat!"

∽

Why shouldn't there be any handicapped jokes?
Because if it weren't for the handicapped, we'd never get parking places.

∽

An unfortunate couple had a son who was born with no legs. What did they name him?
Neil.
Their daughter was born with one leg. What did they name her?
Eileen.

This beautiful young paraplegic was sitting on the beach in her wheelchair, gazing mournfully out at the crashing waves, when a handsome guy came up behind her. "What's wrong?" he asked gently. "Why do you look so sad?"

"I've never been kissed," she explained, brushing a tear off her cheek.

"Well, I can take care of that," said the fellow, and did, then walked off down the beach feeling pretty pleased with himself.

The next week he was walking down the beach again when what should he see but the same beautiful young paraplegic, looking more down-in-the-mouth than ever. "What's wrong now?" he asked, looking deep into her eyes.

"I've never been fucked," she said sadly.

"No problem," he said, his chest swelling with manly pride. He bent over to lift her from the wheelchair, cradled her gently in his arms, and walked slowly down the pier. Reaching the end, he threw her in the water and shouted, "Now you're fucked!"

❦

Did you hear about the nice woman who gave Ray Charles a ticket to see Marcel Marceau?

The Williams were suitably unhappy when their first child was born with no ears, and their best friends, the Cains, were well aware of this. Preparing for their first visit to see the newborn, Mrs. Cain reminded her husband that at all costs he should avoid any reference to the baby's defect.

In no time at all both couples found themselves cooing over the crib. "Look at those arms," said Mrs. Cain. "He's really going to be able to throw a ball. And those legs—he could be a sprinter. Say, how're his eyes?"

"Terrific," said the proud mother.

"They better be," blurted Cain. "He'll never be able to wear glasses!"

❧

A guy was passing through the town on his way across the state when he decided it was time for lunch. He pulled up in front of a little boy sitting on some front steps and asked, "S-s-s-say, k-k-k-kid, d-d-d-you know wh-wh-where I c-c-c-could g-g-get a hot m-m-meal around h-h-here?"

The kid didn't say a word.

"Hey k-k-k-k-kid, d-d-d-don't you know s-s-s-somewhere s-s-s-serving f-f-food around h-h-h-here?"

The kid shook his head, and the tourist drove off in disgust. Just then the boy's mother came out of the house. "Herbie," she said, "you've lived in this town all your life. Don't tell me you don't know somewhere to get a bit of lunch."

"I d-d-d-do," said the kid, "b-b-b-but you th-th-think I w-w-w-wwanna get sl-sl-sl-slapped?"

❧

Then there's the sad story of the poor guy who was in a terrible motorcycle accident. When he came out from under the anesthetic, the doctor was leaning over him anxiously. "Son," he said, "I've got some good news and some bad news. The bad news is that you were in a very serious accident, and I'm afraid we had to amputate both your feet just above the ankle."

"Jesus," gasped the patient. "What's the good news?"

"The fellow in the next bed over would like to buy your boots."

❧

What do you say to a one-legged hitchhiker?
"Hop in!"

A blind man and his friend were walking along with the blind man's dog, when the dog simply raised its leg and pissed on the blind man's shoe. To his friend's astonishment, the man reached over and proceeded to stroke the dog's back.

"What the hell are you patting him for?" exclaimed his friend. "The dog just pissed on you!"

"I gotta find out where his head is," said the blind man testily, "so I can kick his ass."

∽

What do you get when an epileptic falls into a lettuce patch?

Seizure salad.

Jokes for the Blind

More Jokes
for the Blind

Male Anatomy

*T*his fellow married a virgin and wanted to go to special pains to make sure her sexual inexperience wasn't going to be a cause of any tension or trouble. He explained that he didn't ever want her to feel pressured into having sex with him, but wanted it to come of her own free will. "In fact, darling," he said to her tenderly, "I think we should set up a little system in code to make all this as simple as possible. Here's how it'll work: when you want to have sex, pull my penis once; when you don't want to have sex, pull my penis a hundred times."

What did the Pole do before going to the cockfight?
    Greased his zipper.

∾

What's the difference between "ooh" and "aah"?
    About three inches.

∾

What do you get when you cross a rooster and a telephone pole?
    A thirty-foot cock that wants to reach out and touch someone.

∾

Did you hear about the man who couldn't spell?
    He spent the night in a warehouse.

∾

Why can't you circumcise Iranians?
    There's no end to those pricks.

One night after their proprietor was asleep, the parts of the body were arguing about which had the toughest job. "I've really got it rough," bemoaned the feet. "He puts me in these smelly sneakers, makes me jog till I've got blisters . . . it's brutal!"

"You got nothing to complain about," maintained the stomach. "Last night I got nothing but bourbon, pizza, and aspirin. It's a miracle I kept it together."

"Oh quit bitching, you two," moaned the penis. "Every night, I'm telling you, he sticks me in a dark tunnel and makes me do push-ups until I throw up."

❧

There once was a pro football player called Smithers, whose main role was warming the bench. Every game he would put on his pads, smear his cheeks with charcoal, don his helmet and run out onto the field with the rest of the team; but play after play, game after game, season after season went by without Smithers ever being called into action.

One Saturday near the end of the season Smithers was feeling lousy. "Helene," he asked his long-time girl friend, "I want you to do me a favor. Dress up in my uniform, smear your face, put on my helmet, and sit on the bench for me this game. You know I never play, and nobody'll ever know."

Helene required some additional convincing but finally agreed, and sure enough, no one on Smithers's team gave her the time of day. The first half passed without event; she hung out in the locker room during halftime; the third quarter went by smoothly, and it wasn't until the last quarter that one man after another started falling to injuries. The bench grew emptier and emptier and finally, in desperation, the coach barked, "Smithers, get in there!"

Rather panicked, Helene went out onto the field, crouched down in the lineup, and was knocked cold within the first three seconds of play. When she came to, the coach was vigorously massaging her pussy. "Don't worry, Smithers," he said nervously, "once we get your balls back in place, your cock'll pop right up."

~

What's the definition of conceit?

A mosquito with a hard-on floating down the river on his back shouting, "Open the drawbridge!"

~

An international conference of sexologists was convened to determine once and for all why the penis is shaped the way it is. Each national delegation had done extensive research and was to announce its results.

Said the French spokesman, "We have spent five million francs and can now firmly state zat ze penis is ze shape it is in order to give pleasure to ze woman."

"I say," said the British representative, "we've spent thirty thousand pounds and are quite sure that the shape is in order to give maximum pleasure to the man."

"We've spent a million bucks," drawled the American, "and there's no further doubt about the fact that it's that shape so your hand doesn't slip off the end."

⁓

What's the dumbest part of a man?

His prick. (It's got no brains, its best friends are two nuts, and it lives next door to an asshole.)

⁓

When Paddy O'Brian died, Father Flannigan was there to console the bereaved widow. "You know, Molly, the whole community is here to help you through this time of sorrow," he said, "and of course you know I'll do anything I can for you."

Parting her veil and drying her tear-stained cheeks, the widow whispered a single request in Father Flannigan's ear. The priest blushed scarlet and refused outright, but the widow continued her pleas and finally he gave in. He left, saying, "Give me twenty-four hours."

The next day he showed up at the house with something in a brown paper bag.

The widow popped the contents into a pot on the stove, and it was boiling away when a neighbor dropped by. "I say, Molly," said the neighbor opening the lid, "isn't that Paddy's penis?"

"Indeed it is," said Molly. "All his life I had to eat it his way, and now I'm eating it mine."

∾

How can a real man tell when his girl friend's having an orgasm?

Real men don't care.

∾

What's a guy with a 12-inch cock have for breakfast?

Well, this morning I had two eggs over easy, whole wheat toast, and coffee . . .

∾

What has a thousand teeth and eats wienies?

A zipper.

∾

What do you get when you cross a penis and a potato?

A dicktater.

Did you hear about the guy who got his vasectomy done at Sears?

Every time he gets a hard-on, the garage door goes up.

❧

A woman sought the advice of a sex therapist, confiding that she found it increasingly difficult to find a man who could satisfy her, and that it was very wearisome getting in and out of all these short-term relationships. "Isn't there some way to judge the size of a man's equipment from the outside?" she asked earnestly.

"The only foolproof way," counseled the therapist, "is by the size of his feet."

So the woman went downtown and proceeded to cruise the streets, until she came across a young fellow standing in an unemployment line with the biggest feet she had ever laid eyes on. She took him out to dinner, wined and dined him, and then took him back to her apartment for an evening of abandon.

When the man woke up the next morning, the woman had already gone out. By the bedside table was a $20 bill and a note that read, "With my compliments, take this money and go out and buy a pair of shoes that fit you."

What's the difference between anxiety and panic?

Anxiety is the first time you can't do it a second time, and panic is the second time you can't do it the first time.

∾

This 600-pound guy decides he can't go on living this way, so he seeks the help of a clinic and proceeds to go on a drastic diet. It works: four months later he's down to 160 pounds and feeling great, except for one problem. He's covered with great folds of flesh where the fat used to be.

He calls up the clinic, and the doctor tells him not to worry. "There's a special surgical procedure to correct this condition," the doctor assures him. "Just come on over to the clinic."

"But doctor," says the one-time fatty, "you don't understand. I'm too embarrassed to be seen in public like this."

"Don't give it another thought," says the doctor. "Simply pull up all the folds as high as they'll go, pile the flesh on top of your head, put on a top hat, and come on over."

The guy follows the instructions and provokes no comments until he reaches the clinic and is standing in front of the admitting nurse's desk, dying of self-consciousness.

"The doctor will be right with you," says the nurse.

"Say, what's that hole in the middle of your fore-head?"

"My belly button," blurts out the guy, "how d'ya like my tie?"

∽

Did you hear about the flasher who decided to retire?
Yeah, but he changed his mind and decided to stick it out another year.

∽

The newlyweds had never slept together and were most eager to consummate their union. The bride in her eagerness insisted on undressing the groom, but stopped dead upon removing his shoes and socks, finding his toes grossly misshapen.

"Not to worry," the groom explained. "A case of toelio when I was a child."

The bride procceded apace, only to stop again with an expression of shock on her face once she had taken off his pants.

"Nothing but a childhood case of kneesles," he reassured her.

Down to the basics, she reached for his jockey shorts. "I know, I know," she interrupted before her husband could say a word, "nothing but a case of smallcox."

What did the elephant say to the naked man?
"How d'you breathe through that thing?"

~

Why did God give black men such huge pricks?
Because he was so sorry about what he'd done to their hair.

~

What's long and hard and full of semen?
A submarine.

~

What did the egg say to the boiling water?
"How can you expect me to get hard so fast? I just got laid a minute ago!"

~

What was the first thing Adam said to Eve?
"Stand back! I don't know how big this thing gets!"

What do you get when you cross a rooster with a peanut-butter sandwich?

A cock that sticks to the roof of your mouth.

∽

What do you get when you cross a rooster with an owl?

A cock that stays up all night.

∽

A man came into a bar, sat down at the bar for a drink, and noticed that there was a horse in the back of the room with a big pot of money in front of it. "What's that all about?" he asked the bartender.

"You gotta put a dollar in the pot," explained the bartender, "and you collect the pot if you can make the horse laugh."

The guy went over to the horse, whispered in its ear, and the horse cracked up, fell over, and rolled on the floor in laughter. And the fellow picked up the pot and walked out.

Five years later the same guy walked into the same bar and saw the same horse at the back with another big pot of money in front of it. "It's not so easy," said the bartender. "This time you gotta make the horse *cry*."

The guy walked over to the horse, and in a matter of minutes the horse fell to its knees, sobbing as though its heart were breaking. The guy picked up the pot and was on his way out the door when the bartender stopped him.

"Hey," he said, "at least tell us how you did it."

"Easy," said the guy. "The first time I told him my prick was bigger than his, and the second time I showed him."

∽

The routine practice of circumcision was part of a certain doctor's job, and he found himself reluctant to throw the foreskins away after the operation. So he saved them all up in a jar of formaldehyde. Many years went by, the time came for the doctor to retire from practice, and when cleaning out his office he came across the jar, which by this time contained hundreds of foreskins. It seemed a pity to throw them out after all this time, so, certain that they could be put to some use, he took them down to the tailor around the corner and asked that he make something with them.

"No problem," said the tailor. "Come back in a week."

A week later the tailor proudly presented the doctor with a wallet. "Now wait just a minute!" protested the doctor. "There were literally hundreds of foreskins in that jar, and all I've got to show for it is a measly *wallet?*"

"Relax," said the tailor. "You rub it for a little bit, and it turns into a briefcase."

A black couple took their young son for his first visit to the circus, and by chance their seats were next to the elephant pen. When his father got up to buy some popcorn, the boy piped up, "Mom, what's that long thing on the elephant?"

"That's the elephant's trunk, dear," she replied.

"No, not *that*."

"Oh, that's the elephant's tail."

"No, Mom. Down underneath!"

His mother blushed and said, "Oh, that's nothing." Pretty soon the father returned, and the mother went off to get a soda. As soon as she had left, the boy repeated his question.

"That's the elephant's trunk, son."

"Dad, I *know* what an elephant's trunk is. The thing at the other end."

"Oh, that's the elephant's tail."

"*No*. Down *there*."

The father took a good look and explained, "That's the elephant's penis."

"Dad, how come when I asked Mom, she said it was nothing?"

The man took a deep breath and replied, "Son, I've *spoiled* that woman."

∽

What's the new Webster's definition of "small?"

"Is it in yet?"

Why does a dog lick his balls?
Because he can.

❧

What do you have when you have two little green balls in your hand?
Kermit's undivided attention.

❧

A Polish couple wants a black baby more than anything in the world, but all their efforts come to nothing. Finally, one day they're walking down the street when they spot a black couple with a beautiful black child in a stroller. So they walk over, explain their greatest desire, and ask the blacks for the secret.

"For one thing," says the black man, "you gotta be eight inches long."

"No problem," says the Pole.

"For another," the black goes on, "you gotta be at least three and a half inches around."

"So *that's* the problem!" exclaims the Pole, turning to his wife. "We've been letting too much light in!"

❧

Did you hear about the masochist who said to her boyfriend, "Give me nine inches and make it hurt."
He fucked her twice and slapped her.

This young man decided that, physically, he simply wasn't adequately endowed. Deciding to take matters into his own hands, he went to a doctor and announced his desire to have his penis surgically enlarged.

The doctor checked things out and told the young man that the only real improvement that could be surgically worked was to implant a section of a baby elephant's trunk.

Rather a radical solution, agreed the patient, but he was adamant. The operation was performed without any complications, and after a few weeks of recuperation the young man decided it was time to try out his new accoutrement.

He asked a lovely young woman of his acquaintance out to dinner at an elegant restaurant. They were having a quiet conversation when his new organ, which had been comfortably resting in his left pants leg, whipped out over the table, grabbed a hard roll, and just as speedily disappeared from sight.

"Wow!" said the girl, truly impressed. "Can you do that again?"

"Sure," said the fellow, "but I don't know if my asshole can stand another hard roll."

❦

Three guys were having an argument about who was more generously endowed. Finally, to settle the matter once and for all, they went up to the top of the

Empire State Building and proceeded to unzip their flies.

"Pretty good, huh," said Mort, whose cock was hanging all the way down to the fifty-seventh floor.

"I got you beat cold," said Bill, whose cock was dangling just below a window on the forty-ninth.

They looked over at the third guy, who was dancing a curious sort of jig, jumping from one foot to the other and peering anxiously over the edge of the observation deck.

"What the hell are you doing, Harry?" they asked.

"Dodging traffic," he replied.

∾

It was time for sex-education class, and the teacher asked the class, "Children, who can tell me what breasts are?"

"My Mommy has breasts," piped up Rhonda. "She has two of them."

"Right you are, Rhonda," praised the teacher. "Now who can tell me what a penis is?"

"I know," said Eric. "My Daddy has two of them."

"Are you sure?" asked the teacher, puzzled.

"Uh huh," said Eric. "One's about this long," holding his hands about four inches apart, "and looks like mine, and the other's about this long," holding his hands about seven inches apart, "and he uses it to brush Mommy's teeth with."

What's hard and straight going in, and soft and sticky coming out?

Chewing gum.

❧

Two guys were sitting on a bridge passing the time of day and drinking beer, and pretty soon they both had to take a leak. Wanting to impress his companion, the first guy said, "Gee, this water's *cold*."

"And deep," said his friend.

❧

How is a man like a snowstorm?

Because you don't know when he's coming, how many inches you'll get, or how long it'll stay.

❧

What's twelve inches long and white?

Nothing.

Female Anatomy

What you do call a woman who can suck a golf ball through fifty feet of garden hose?
   Darling.

∽

What's the perfect woman?
   A deaf, dumb, and blind nymphomaniac who owns a liquor store.

This well-to-do suburban matron makes an appointment for her annual checkup with a new gynecologist. Following the examination, he ushers her into his office to give her the results. "You'll be glad to hear that everything is absolutely in order," he says, leaning forward with a smile. "In fact, you have the cleanest vagina I've ever seen."

"It should be," she snaps. "I've got a colored man coming in twice a week."

A young lady went out on a date with a young man she found quite attractive, so after dinner and the movies she invited him back to her apartment. Sitting him down on her couch with a drink, she proceeded to nibble on his ear, play with his hair, and so on, but the fellow only pulled up his collar and rubbed his hands together for warmth. The young lady pulled out all the stops, sitting on his lap, even directing his hands to appropriate portions of her anatomy. But he took no action whatsoever and violently resisted her efforts to unbutton even a single one of his outer garments.

Finally in desperation, after a particularly passionate kiss had met with no response, she said, "You know, I have a hole down here."

"Oh," he said with evident relief, "so that's where the draft is coming from!"

It was late at night, and the tired cabbie was on his last run of the night. Reaching the destination, he said to the little old lady in the back seat, "That'll be eight bucks, please.

There was no answer, so thinking her hearing might be at fault, he said loudly, "Lady, the fare is eight bucks."

Still no response. So he turned around, only to be greeted by the sight of the elderly woman hoisting her skirts and spreading her legs, no underwear impairing his view.

"Well, sonny," she cackled, "will this be payment enough?"

"Aw, lady," he sighed, "doncha have anything smaller?"

ᧁ

What do you call a JAP's nipple?
　　The tip of the iceberg.

ᧁ

Why do women like hunters?
　　Three reasons:
　　They go deep into the bush.
　　They always shoot twice.
　　And they always eat what they shoot.

This middle-aged woman decides she's not getting any younger and that it's time to spice up her sex life. Since she has always had a crush on the Beatles, she goes to the local tattooist with a very specific request. "I would like John Lennon tattooed on the inside of my right thigh, looking up," she instructs him, "and Paul McCartney on the left thigh, looking up. Now, are you sure you can handle this?"

The tattooist assures her that he's the best in the business, and sets to work.

A week or two later, the recuperation period is over. The woman takes off the bandages and goes over to her mirror in great anticipation, only to discover that to her horror the two portraits bear no resemblance at all to Lennon and McCartney. She rushes over to the tattooist's office in a rage.

"I don't see what you're complaining about," he says soothingly. "I think the likenesses are astonishing. But clearly we need a third, unbiased opinion." So he goes out to the sidewalk and brings back the first person he encounters, a wino still reeling from the night before. Confronting him with the evidence, the tattooist asks the wino, "Now on that right side, does that look like John Lennon?"

"I dunno," says the wino after a long silence.

"Well, how about the left one?" asks the tattooist. "Is that or is that not the spitting image of Paul McCartney?"

"I dunno," says the wino after considerable thought. "But that guy in the middle with the beard and the bad breath, that's *gotta* be Willie Nelson."

What's the only thing used sanitary napkins are good for?

Tea bags for vampires.

∿

Why does it take women longer to climax?

Who cares?

∿

How can you tell if a Polish woman is having her period?

She's only wearing one sock.

∿

What's the latest disease in Poland?

Toxic Sock Syndrome!

∿

Three guys were sitting around in a bar discussing whose wife was the most frigid. Harry was definitely sure he had the worst of it. "Listen, you guys," he said, "my wife comes to bed with an ice cube in each hand, and in the morning they haven't begun to melt."

"That's *nothing*," said Phil. "My wife likes to have a glass of water on the bedside table, but by the time she's carried it from the bathroom to the bedroom, it's frozen solid.

"Aw, hell," said Herb, "my wife is so frigid that when she spreads her legs, the furnace kicks on."

❧

What's the difference between a magician and a chorus line?

A magician has cunning feats and stunts.

❧

God has just spent six days creating the heavens and the earth, and since it's the seventh day of rest, He and Gabriel are sitting back and admiring His handiwork.

"You know, God," says Gabriel, "you have done one hell of a job—excuse my language. Those snowy peaks are unbelievably majestic, and the woods, with those little sunny dells and meadows . . . masterful. Not to mention the oceans: those fantastic coral reefs and all the sea creatures and the waves crashing on the beaches. And all the animals—from fleas to elephants—what a job. Not to mention the heavens; how could I leave them out? What a touch, that Milky Way."

God beams.

"I just have the smallest suggestion, if you'll excuse my presumption," says Gabriel. "You know those sample humans you put down there in the Garden of Eden?"

God nods, a frown furrowing His brow.

"Well," says Gabriel, "I was just wondering whether, for all the obvious reasons, they shouldn't have differing sets of genitalia as all the other animals do?"

God reflects on this for a minute, and then a smile crosses His face. "You're right," He exclaims. "Give the dumb one a cunt!"

❧

When you order a Bloody Mary, how can you tell if the waitress is mad at you?

She leaves the string in.

❧

Why do women rub their eyes when they get out of bed in the morning?

Because they don't have balls to scratch.

❧

Mrs. Smith was quite embarrassed when little Johnny burst into the shower, pointed at her pubic hair, and asked loudly, "What's that, Mommy?"

"That's my sponge, honey," she explained.

She was even more embarrassed when Johnny burst in a week later, because, to satisfy one of Mr. Smith's kinkier requests, she had shaved herself. In answer to Johnny's question, she hastily explained that she had lost her sponge. "It got dirty, honey, and I threw it out the window."

Johnny was gone for a couple of hours, but came back with a big grin on his face. "I found your sponge, Mommy," he cried. "I looked in the Browns' window, and Mrs. Brown was washing Mr. Brown's face with it!"

༄

There was great excitement in the laboratory when the eminent scientist announced a new invention—the apple. That was nothing new, his colleagues pointed out; the apple had been around for a long time.

"Yes, but this apple tastes like pussy," proudly explained the scientist. "Try it."

A skeptical fellow took a big bite, only to spit it out all over the floor. "It tastes like *shit*," he said disgustedly.

"Indeed," said the scientist. "Turn it around."

༄

What's the function of a woman?

Life-support system for a pussy.

What do you call a truckload of vibrators?
    Toys for twats.

∾

The elementary school lesson for the day was The Farm. "All right, children," said the teacher, "who can tell me the name of the big building all the animals sleep in?"

"The barn," piped up Melissa.

"Very good, Melissa. And who knows the name of the tall, cylindrical building next to the barn that the farmer stores the grain in?"

"The silo," said Susie.

"Right, Susie. And who knows what the little metal bird up on the roof of the barn is called, class? Mark?"

"That's . . . uh . . . the weather-thing."

"Well, you're right, Mark, it is for telling us something about the weather. But who can tell us what the exact name is, and why?"

"It's a weathercock," explained Davey, "because if it were a weathercunt the wind would blow right through it."

∾

How can you tell if a woman is wearing panty-hose?
    If her ankles swell up when she farts.

Why are hockey goaltenders and Polish girls alike?
They both change their pads after three periods.

◆

Did you hear about the Italian girl who thought a sanitary belt was a drink from a clean shot glass?

◆

Cinderella is thrilled about her invitation to the ball, but her feelings soon turn to dismay when she realizes she has nothing but rags to wear. "Don't worry," says her fairy godmother, and—*Poof*—a beautiful gown and sparkling pair of slippers instantly appear. "But there's a condition," warns the godmother as Cinderella preens in front of the mirror. "You must be home by midnight or your pussy will turn into a pumpkin."

The dazzling Cinderella soon captures the heart of the most handsome man at the ball, and they are dancing rapturously—until Cinderella remembers to look at her watch. "Oh my God," she gasps. "It's almost midnight! I must be going." But the young man runs after her as she makes for the door, begging her to stay and insisting that she at least give him her name so that he can find her again.

"My name is Cinderella," she says. "What's yours?"

"Peter Peter Pumpkin Eater," says he.

"Oh, in *that* case I'll stay."

Harry was delighted when he found a young woman who accepted his proposal of marriage, as he was sensitive about his wooden leg and a bit afraid no one would have him. In fact, he couldn't bring himself to tell his fiancée about his leg when he slipped the ring on her finger, nor when she bought the dress, nor when they picked the time and place. All he kept saying was, "Darling, I've got a big surprise for you," at which she blushed and smiled bewitchingly.

The wedding itself came and went, and the young couple were at last alone in their hotel room. "Now don't forget, Harry, you promised me a big surprise," said the bride.

Unable to say a word, Harry turned out the lights, unstrapped his wooden leg, slipped into bed, and placed his wife's hand on the stump.

"Hmmmmm," she said softly, "that *is* a surprise. But pass me the Vaseline, and I'll see what I can do."

༄

Fred's wife refused to wear underwear, and it drove him crazy. He didn't think it was proper or sanitary or right, but nothing he said persuaded her to mend her ways. But when she caught a bad cold one winter, Fred had a brainstorm. Calling up the family doctor, he said, "Doc, I wish you'd come and look in on my wife; she's got a terrible cold. And there's something else you could do for me. You see, she's got this terrible habit of going around without any underwear on, and if you could somehow persuade her that the cold was linked to that, why, I'd pay you double."

The doctor came right over and found the woman wrapped in a blanket on the living room sofa, blowing her nose. Looking down her throat, the doctor said, "Mrs. Brown, I'll give you something for this cold . . . but if you don't start wearing underpants, it's going to bother you all winter."

"You mean to tell me, doctor," she said, "that you can tell from looking down my throat that I'm not wearing panties?"

"That's right," he assured her.

"Well then, would you mind looking up my asshole and letting me know if my hat's on straight?"

∾

This couple is lying in bed one morning, and she takes it in mind to tell him the dream she had the night before. "Honey, I dreamed I was at a cock auction: there were extra-large cocks going for $90 or so, medium-size cocks selling for $50, and itty-bitty ones for $1.50."

"Say, was mine in the auction?" the man inquires a bit anxiously.

"Honey, yours would've been too big to get in the door."

A couple of days later they're lying in bed again, and the man says, "You wouldn't believe what I dreamed last night: that I was at a pussy auction.

There were great big ones, and little hairy ones, oh, all kinds."

"Well, did you see mine?" she asks.

"Baby," he says, "the auction was *in* your pussy."

⌇

The divorce case was an especially acrimonious one, as the wife was suing on the grounds that her husband had completely failed to satisfy her. "Frankly," she advised the court in a stage whisper, "he was so poorly endowed—and I mean tiny—that it just wasn't even worth the effort."

The sympathetic judge awarded a large cash settlement to the woman, and as she left the stand and walked past her husband, she hissed, "So long, sucker."

Sticking a finger in each corner of his mouth and pulling it as wide as possible, he said, "So long, bitch."

⌇

What do soybeans and dildos have in common?
    They're both meat substitutes.

⌇

What do eating pussy and the Mafia have in common?
    One slip of the tongue and you're in deep shit.

What's worse than getting raped by Jack the Ripper?
Getting fingered by Captain Hook.

❧

Why is it so groovy to be a test-tube baby?
Because you've got a womb with a view.

❧

Mel and Howie are frequent fishing partners, but Howie always catches more fish than Mel. One Saturday morning they're out on the lake, and Howie's pulled in a couple of nice-sized bass. Mel notices Howie sniffing his bait before putting it on the hook.

"How come?" he asks his friend.

"I have this friend who works in an autopsy room," explains Howie, "and he slips me the cunts. They make great bait."

"I can see that," says Mel. "But why do you smell them?"

"Every so often he slips in an asshole."

❧

Why did a fellow trade in his wife for an outhouse?
The hole was smaller and the smell was better.

There was this girl who lived in New Jersey, and she loved it so much that she named parts of her body after places in the Garden State. One night she confided this to her boyfriend as he was beginning to feel up her right tit. "I bet you call this Mount Pleasant," he said, and she smiled in assent.

Working his hand down her ass, he asked, "And this?"

"I call that Freehole," said she.

Getting hot and heavy, he maneuvered his hand around to the front. "I bet you call this Cherry Hill," he said triumphantly.

"Nope. That's Eatontown."

૭✺

Why do women have two holes so close together?

In case you miss.

૭✺

If God hadn't meant us to eat pussy, He wouldn't have made it look like a taco.

Did you hear about the bride who was so horny she carried a bouquet of batteries?

～

A young man was raised in the Australian outback by his father alone, who, not wanting him to get into any trouble, told him to stay away from women. "They have teeth down there," he explained, and let the impressionable boy's imagination do the rest.

In time, however, the fellow's father died. He saw friends getting married and starting families, and he decided it was time to get on with it. So he found himself a willing girl—who was rather disappointed when the consummation consisted of a peck on the cheek alone. The second night she dolled herself up in her sheerest negligée, only to find that once again he pecked her on the cheek, rolled over, and went to sleep. On the third night she caught him before the snores began and proceeded to give him a brief lecture on the birds and the bees and his conjugal duties.

"Oh, no, you don't!" the new husband cried. "I know about you women. You've got teeth down there, and I ain't coming anywhere near."

Well, the bride roared with laughter and invited her husband around the bed for a close inspection. Cautiously he came over and proceeded to look things over with great care. Finally he stuck up his head.

"You're right," he proclaimed. "You've got no teeth, and your gums are in terrible condition!"

Harry came into work on Monday feeling absolutely fine, and so was astonished when his secretary urged him to lie down on the sofa; even more so when his boss took one look at him and ordered him to take the day, if not the week, off. Even his poker buddies wouldn't have anything to do with him, insisting he go straight to bed. Finally, tired of resisting everyone's advice, he went to see his doctor, who took one look at him and rushed over with a stretcher.

"But doctor," he protested, "I *feel* fine."

Well, this was a puzzler, conceded the doctor, who proceeded to refer to the enormous reference tomes behind his desk, muttering to himself. "Looks good, feels good . . . No, you look like hell. Looks good, feels terrible . . . Nah, you feel fine, right?" Thumbing furiously through another volume, he said, "Looks terrible, feels terrible . . . Nope, that won't do it either." Finally, "Looks terrible, feels terrific . . . Aha! You're a vagina!"

❧

Did you hear why Polish women can't use vibrators?
   They chip their teeth.

❧

What's the difference between parsley and pussy?
   Nobody eats *parsley*.

Did you hear about the new New Wave band called
the Toxic Shock Syndrome?

Their new hit's called "Ragtime."

∾

What's green and slimy and smells like Miss Piggy?

Kermit's finger.

∾

It was a hot summer day in the ghetto, and a bunch
of little kids were sitting around with no money, nowhere to go, nothing to do. Until someone's dad stuck
his head out the window, gave some money to his
kid, and told them to get lost and have a good time.

The kid dashed down the block with the others
running after him and, much to their astonishment,
disappeared into the corner drugstore. After a few
minutes he emerged, carrying something in a paper
bag. His friends crowded around, demanding to see
what he'd bought with the money, and were not at
all pleased to see him pull out a box of Tampax.

"Hey, man," they groaned, "we wanted to go out
and find ourselves a good time with that money.
Why'd you go an' buy *that* shit fo'?"

"Dat's why I *got* it," the boy explained. "It say
right here on the box: You can go swimmin', you can
go horseback riding . . ."

How can you tell a Pole designed the lower half of a woman's anatomy?

Who else would put the shithole so close to the snack bar?

You know how these days everyone wants a second opinion? Well, this lady had been going to a psychiatrist for years, and one day she decided she'd had enough of it. "Doctor," she said, walking into his office, "I've been seeing you every week for five years now. I don't feel any better; I don't feel any worse—What's the story? I want you to level with me: What's wrong with me?"

"Well," said the doctor, "I'll tell you. "You're crazy."

"Now wait just a minute," the woman protested. "I want a second opinion."

"Okay," said the doctor. "You're ugly, too."

On the eve of her wedding the bride-to-be confessed to her best friend that—unbeknownst to her fiancé—she was not a virgin. "No problem," said the friend. "Go out and buy a nice piece of liver and put it up inside you before the time comes. You'll feel nice and tight, and he'll never know the difference."

So the bride went ahead with the plan, and on the wedding night the couple went crazy: They fucked on the floor, on the kitchen table, in the bathroom, in the bed. So the bride was truly astonished to wake up the next morning to find her new husband gone, the only trace of him a note on the bedside table. "Dearest," it read, "I love you very much, but I've realized we can't go on like this and can never have a life together. Farewell. P.S. Your vagina is in the sink."

～

Why do tampons have strings?
　　So you can floss after you eat.

～

What's red and has seven little dents in it?
　　Snow White's cherry.

～

This guy walks into a bar and says to the bartender, "I'll have a bourbon and water . . . and get that douche bag down there whatever she'd like to drink," motioning toward a young woman sitting at the other end of the bar.

"Listen, buddy," says the bartender, "this is a family place, and I'll thank you not to use that sort of language in here."

"Okay, okay," says the guy, "just get me a bourbon and water and get that douche bag a drink too."

"That's a perfectly nice young lady," sputters the bartender, "and—"

"I'm getting thirsty," interrupts the guy, "and you better hurry up with the douche bag's order."

The bartender gives up and moves down the bar, rather shamefacedly asking the woman, "The gentleman at the bar would like to offer you a drink—What'll you have?"

"Vinegar and water, thanks," she replies.

૭৲

Do you know why women have cunts?
So men will talk to them.

૭৲

This guy and girl are making out in the back seat of the car, and things are getting pretty hot and heavy. "Put your finger inside me," she asks, and he's only too happy to oblige.

"Put another finger inside me," she orders, moaning in pleasure.

"Put your whole hand inside me."

"Put both hands inside me."

"Now clap."

"I can't!" the guy protests.

"Tight, huh?" she smiles.

How do you fuck a fat girl?
　　Roll her in flour and go for the wet spot.

～

　Two women are sitting on the front stoop, passing the time. "Damnit," says one to the other, "my husband came home with a dozen roses. I'm gonna have to spend all weekend with my legs in the air."
　"Why?" asks her friend. "Don't you have a vase?"

～

Why do women have two holes?
　　So that when they're drunk, you can carry them like a six-pack.

～

What did the blind man say as he passed the fish market?
　　"Good morning, girls."

～

What's the difference between garbage and a girl from New Jersey?
　　Sometimes garbage gets picked up.

How can you tell if your girlfriend's too fat?
 If she sits on your face and you can't hear the stereo.

❧

What do Picasso and Princess Anne have in common?
 Blue periods.

❧

"Ya got no tits and a tight box," snarled the guy to his girlfriend.
 "Get off my back!" she snapped.

❧

Why's pubic hair curly?
 You'd poke your eye out if it were straight.

❧

What's the difference between a nymphomaniac and a lover?
 A lover stops to eat.

Why do women slap Polish midgets?
　　Because they're always telling them how nice their hair smells.

～

Why don't they let women swim in the ocean any more?
　　They can't get the smell out of the fish.

～

How can you tell when a Polish woman's not wearing any underwear?
　　By the dandruff on her shoes.

～

What do control-top pantyhose and Brooklyn have in common?
　　Flatbush.

～

Did you hear about the blind gynecologist?
　　He could read lips.

"There's a new feminine-hygiene spray out on the market," confided Sandra to Denise at Denise's Tupperware party. "It's called SSY."

"Oh yeah?" said Denise. "How come?"

"That's what you get when you take the PU out of pussy."

⤶

What has eighteen legs and two tits?
    The Supreme Court.

⤶

A doctor was performing a routine gynecological examination when he happened upon a teabag. When he asked his patient about it, she looked up in horror and exclaimed, "Oh my God! Then what could I have put in the hot water?"

⤶

There was once a young man who was fixated on the female breast, and he decided to seek professional help. The first test his new psychotherapist performed was one of simple word-association. "Simply say the first word that comes into your mind," the doctor explained. "Orange."

"Breast," said the young man without hesitation.

"Plum," said the doctor.

"Breast," said the young man.

"Grapefruit," said the doctor.

"Breast," said the young man.

"Windshield wipers," said the doctor.

"Breast," said the young man.

"Now just hold on a second," said the doctor. "Oranges I can see reminding you of breasts. Plums, maybe; grapefruit if you're stretching it. But windshield wipers?"

"Sure," said the young man. "First this one, then that one . . ."

∾

There was a promiscuous young couple making out in the back seat of a car. Temperatures were rising and things were getting pretty intense, and finally the girl gasped, "Oh darling, darling, kiss me where it smells."

So he drove her to New Jersey.

∾

What's the difference between a bowling ball and pussy?

You can only fit three fingers in a bowling ball.

Why did God invent booze?
  So that fat, ugly girls could have a chance to get
  laid, too.

ᴖ

Why do little Polish girls put fish in their underwear?
  So they'll smell like big Polish girls.

ᴖ

A young couple was making out feverishly on her
parents' sofa a few days before their wedding. "Oh
baby," moaned the groom-to-be, "please let me see your
breasts. I just wanna look." His fiancée blushed and
protested, but unbuttoned her shirt.

"Oh honey," he moaned, "let me kiss them."

"Don't you think we should wait till the wedding?"
she asked, but it was already too late.

Pretty soon he was begging her to take off her panties. "I just wanna look, I swear," he panted.

"I really think we should wait till the wedding like
we said we would," she said, but was finally persuaded
by the fact that he was just going to look.

Well, she was adamant about not letting him kiss
her down there, insisting that was something special
they should wait for. But after a good half hour of art-
ful argument, he had his way. Only to stick his head
up a moment later and say anxiously, "Baby, you
think that'll *keep* till Sunday?"

Why did God create women?
    Because sheep can't cook.

~

What's a perfect 10?
    A woman about waist-high with no teeth and a
    flat head you can rest your drink on.

~

What's a Cinderella 10?
    A woman who sucks and fucks till midnight and
    then turns into a pizza and a six-pack.

~

Did you hear about the new feminine-hygiene prod-
uct?
    It's called Toxic Shock Absorbers.

Homosexual

Did you hear about the Polish lesbian?
She likes men.

~

What do you call a Jewish homosexual?
He-blew.
What do you call an Irish homosexual?
Gay-lick.
What do you call a Chinese homosexual?
Chew-man-chew.
What do you call an Italian homosexual?
A Guinea cocksucker.

A gay riding along in the subway saw a good-looking man sitting opposite him and was instantly smitten. Following him out of the station, he trailed him into an office building and up to an office. What luck! The man was a proctologist, and he signed up for an appointment. But when the examination progressed, the gay's squeals of evident pleasure infuriated the doctor. His job was to cure illnesses, not to titillate, and making that perfectly clear, he tossed the gay guy out.

The gay, however, was really in love and soon telephoned the doctor's office again, claiming a genuine medical problem and insisting on his services. The doctor reluctantly consented to another office visit. Examining the man, he was astonished to find a long green stem, thorns attached, and then another, then another.

"My God," the doctor cried, "you've got a dozen red roses up your ass! Now I warned you, I'm a reputable doctor. Are you up to the same old tricks again?"

"Read the card," gasped the gay, "read the card!"

Two gay guys were talking when one leaned over and said to the other, "You know, I just got circumcised two weeks ago."

"How wonderful," gasped his friend. "You must let me see it."

The first man obliged, pulling down his pants and proudly displaying his cock.

"Ooooh!" shrieked his friend. "You look ten years younger!"

◡

How do you fit four gays at a crowded bar?
　　Turn the stool upside down.

◡

There are these two gay guys who decide they want to have a baby. So they find an obliging lesbian, have her impregnated by sperm donation, and are simply thrilled when she gives birth to a seven-pound baby boy. They rush to the hospital for the first viewing of their son, standing with their noses pressed against the glass of the nursery window and surveying row upon row of squalling infants. Except for one quiet, clean little baby, cooing softly to itself amid all the chaos.

Sure enough, when the gays ask to see their son, the nurse heads for the quiet baby and brings him over for the proud parents to ogle.

"Gee," said one of them to the nurse, "he sure is well behaved compared to the rest of those howling brats, isn't he?"

"Oh, he's quiet now," said the nurse, "but he squalls like all the rest when I take the pacifier out of his ass."

Two gay guys, Larry and Phil, were driving down the highway when they were rear-ended by a huge semi. Somewhat shaken, they maneuvered over to the side of the road, where Phil instructed Larry to get out and confront the truck driver. "Tell him we're going to sue, sue, sue!" he shrieked.

Obligingly Larry got out and went around to the cab of the truck to deliver this message to the huge, burly driver, whose response was to snarl, "Ah, why doncha suck my cock."

"Phil," said Larry coming back to their car, "I think we're going to be able to settle out of court."

❧

What do you call a lesbian Eskimo?
  A Klondike.

❧

How do you identify a bull dyke?
  She kick-starts her vibrator and rolls her own tampons.

❧

What do you get when you cross a gay Eskimo and a black?
  A snowblower that doesn't work.

This guy is taking a leak in a public men's room when a man enters with his arms held out from his sides, bent at the elbows with his hands dangling awkwardly, and comes over to him. "Would you do me a favor and unzip my fly?" he asks.

Figuring the man to be a poor cripple, perhaps an accident victim, the guy obliges, not without a flush of embarrassment when the man next requests that he take out his prick and hold it in the appropriate position.

"Shake it off" is the next instruction, then "zip me up," and the guy follows orders, wincing at his own embarrassment and at the shame of being so helpless.

"Say, thanks," says the man, flouncing to the door. "I guess my nails are dry now."

❧

What's the definition of confusion?
     Twenty blind lesbians in a fish market.

❧

What's the definition of a Bloody Mary?
     A wounded faggot.

❧

What do you call a lesbian opera singer?
     A muff diva.

How can you tell when your roommate's gay?
　　When his cock tastes like shit.

～

Did you hear about the gay Catholic?
　　He couldn't decide whether the Pope was fabulous or simply divine.

～

Is it better to be born black or gay?
　　Black, because you don't have to tell your parents.

～

What's this? (Stick out your tongue.)
　　A lesbian with a hard-on.

～

How can you tell if you walk into a gay church?
　　Only half the congregation is kneeling.

Blanche Knott

Did you hear about the queer Indian?
He jumped into a canoe, took three strokes, and shot across the lake.

How about the queer burglar?
He couldn't blow the safe, so he went down on the elevator.

Why don't senators use bookmarks?
They just bend over the pages.

Why do gay men have mustaches?
To hide the stretch marks.

What do you call the zipper on a gay Italian's pants?
A Mediterranean fruit fly.

What's the definition of analingus?
 Tongue-in-cheek.

～

Herbie had always done well in school and was doing even better in college, so his parents were a bit surprised to be summoned by the guidance counselor.

"I have some good news and some bad news, Mr. and Mrs. Robinson," said the counselor. "The bad news is that Herbie is gay."

Herbie's parents blanched.

"The good news is that he's going to be Homecoming Queen."

～

What did one lesbian say to another?
 "Your face or mine?"

～

An obviously gay guy swished onto a bus to face a derogatory sneer from the massive bus driver. "Faggot," he growled, "where're your pearls?"

"Pearls with corduroy!" shrieked the gay. "Are you *mad?*"

How many gays does it take to change a light bulb?
Seven. One to change the bulb, and six to shriek,
"Faaaaabulous!"

～

What do Polish lesbians use for a lubricant?
Tartar sauce.

～

Considering that in order to get married, you have to
have a marriage license, what do two lesbians have to
get?
A licker license.

～

What do you call a gay milkman?
A Dairy Queen.

～

Why was the homosexual fired from his job at the
sperm bank?
For drinking on the job.

Religion

*W*hy *doesn't Jesus eat M&Ms?*
>   They keep falling through the holes in his hands.

∽

What did Jesus say to Mary while he was on the cross?
>   "Can you get my flats? These spikes are *killing* me."

∽

Why did they crucify Jesus instead of stoning him to death?
>   Because it's easier to cross yourself than to pound yourself all over. (Note: This joke requires the accompanying gestures.)

Late one night the Pope's most intimate council of senior advisors requests admission to His Holiness's bedchamber, bearing news of the greatest urgency. They tell him that it has just been revealed by sacred divinations that unless the Pope sleeps with a woman, the Vatican State—indeed all of Catholicism—will come to a sudden and terrible end.

The Pope thinks it over for a few minutes, and then agrees to go ahead with the profane deed. "But," he says, "I have three stipulations.

"First, she must be blind, so she cannot see where she is being taken.

"Second, she must be deaf, so she cannot speak of what has happened to her.

"And third, she must have big tits."

❧

Why didn't Jesus get into college?
He got hung up on his boards.

❧

"The question for today, boys and girls," said Sister Mary, "is, 'What part of the body goes to heaven first?'"

Dirty Eddie was sitting in the front row waving his hand wildly, but since his answers were usually less than satisfactory, Sister Mary refrained from calling on him. "Yes, Veronica?"

"The heart, Sister Mary, because that's where God's love touches you."

"Very good," said Sister Mary. "Yes, Marilyn?"

"The soul, Sister Mary, because that's the immortal part of us."

"Very good, Marilyn," said Sister Mary, observing with dismay that Dirty Eddie's hand was still waving. "Yes, Eddie?"

"The feet, Sister, the feet."

"Well, that's a curious answer, Eddie. Why the feet?"

"Because I've seen Ma with her feet up in the air, shouting, 'I'm coming, God, I'm coming!'"

❧

This nice guy dies and goes to heaven, where he is shown to a simple hut, dressed in a plain cotton robe, and offered wine and cheese. He had anticipated something a little fancier but all his needs are cared for, so he settles in happily . . . until, on his daily stroll, he comes across a fellow he had known on earth to be a scoundrel and criminal. This fellow is lounging on a luxurious cloud with a gorgeous blonde, dressed in a sumptuous toga, and is holding a bottle of Chivas Regal.

All upset, the nice guy goes to talk to St. Peter. "Listen, St. Peter, on earth I was a great guy, never hurt anyone, never cheated, never stole, and all I get in heaven is a grass hut and some cheap wine. And there's this guy who lied to his mother, stole from his brother, and tortured his sister, living in the lap of luxury. It's not fair!"

"It's not all it's cut out to be, my son," smiles St. Peter. "He's got a bottle of scotch with a hole in it and a beautiful blonde without one."

∽

How do you know Christ wasn't born in Italy?

They couldn't find three wise men and a virgin.

∽

A white guy and a black guy were having an argument as to whether God was white or black. So they booked a flight to the Holy Land, trekked up Mt. Sinai, and shouted their question up toward the sky as loudly as possible.

"I AM WHAT I AM," boomed down the earth-shaking response.

"You *see*," said the white guy, turning around to his friend triumphantly.

"Whaddaya mean?" asked the black guy. "What does that prove?"

"Listen, if He were black, he would have said, 'I is what I is.' "

This Irish lawyer dies and arrives at the Pearly Gates at the same time as the Pope. The Pope is assigned to a hovel and given a dry crust of bread, while the lawyer is ushered into a huge mansion where a staff of servants is placed at his disposal.

"What's the story?" the Pope angrily demands of St. Peter. "I was the head of the whole Catholic church and I'm stuck in a hovel, and you give this lawyer the run of the place . . ."

"Well, your Holiness," gently explained St. Peter, "we have literally hundreds of Popes here in heaven, but we've never had an Irish lawyer before."

❧

Moses and Jesus are out fishing on the Sea of Galilee and the conversation comes around to miracles. "I'd sure like to perform one," says Moses, "but I'm a bit out of shape—it's been 4000 years since my last one." Jesus urges him on, so Moses goes up to the bow of the boat, raises both arms out above the waters, and commands them to part. With a great roar, the sea parts to reveal a seabed dry as a bone, then comes together again at Moses' second command. "Not bad, eh?" says Moses, settling back down in the stern. "Think you can match that?"

"No problem," says Jesus. "After all it's only been 2000 years since this last trick." He jumps nimbly up onto the gunwale of the boat and steps gracefully out onto the water—only to sink like a stone. Moses hauls him aboard, choking and sputtering, and Jesus insists on trying again, but with the same ignominious result.

With considerable difficulty Moses gets Jesus aboard the second time, and can barely keep from laughing at the dejected heap on the bottom of the boat. "I don't know what it could be," says Jesus sadly, "except the first time around I didn't have these holes in my feet . . ."

❧

A naive young priest is moved to a parish in a bad neighborhood of Manhattan and is quite bewildered by the legion of hookers who are constantly approaching him to whisper, "Five bucks for a blow job, buddy."

Finally he can stand being in ignorance no longer, and approaches one of the nuns. "Excuse my presumption, Sister," says the young priest, "but could you please tell me what a blow job is?"

"Five bucks, just like anywhere else," she replies.

❧

The Pope is working on a crossword puzzle one Sunday afternoon. He stops for a moment or two, scratches his forehead, then asks the Cardinal, "Can you think of a four-letter word for 'woman' that ends in 'u-n-t?'"

"Aunt," replies the Cardinal.

"Say, thanks," says the Pope. "You got an eraser?"

Mother Theresa comes to New York and is greeted by a welcoming committee that wants to know what in New York she is particularly interested in seeing. "Well, to tell the truth," she says modestly, "I have always wanted to see St. Patrick's Cathedral."

"No problem," assures the head of the committee. "Not only will you see it, we'll clear everyone out and you'll have the whole church to yourself."

At the appointed hour Mother Theresa shows up at the church, where she is ushered in by a respectful prelate and left in solitude. It's only a matter of minutes before God's voice booms down from heaven. "Mother Theresa, you have been an exemplary member of the church all your life, a model for millions. Is there anything, anything at all, that I can do for you while you're here?"

"Actually, yes, there is, God," says Mother Theresa. "I've always wanted to direct."

෴

God gets the word up in heaven that the U.S.A. is a pretty depraved place. Not having the time to spare Himself, He sends Mother Theresa down to earth as His delegate. Her instructions are to visit each of the metropolitan centers and to report back to heaven on what she finds.

The first report isn't long in coming. New York, Mother Theresa says, is filled with unimaginable sin and violence and she is leaving immediately. Boston is no better, however, being full of child molesters, and the cities of the South are no better, with heavy drinkers and sex offenders everywhere. Mother Theresa's next stop is Chicago, but she can't stand the depravity there for more than a few days, and she hops on a plane to Los Angeles.

No words for three weeks. God finally gets concerned, and He gets her number from Information and calls her up. "Terri here," comes on a mellow voice. "I'm not home right now, but if you'd like to share your thoughts . . ."

∾

New slogan: Save Soviet Jewry—Win Valuable Prizes.

∾

What was the Pope's first miracle?
He made a lame man blind.

∾

What was the Pope's second miracle?
He walked under water.

What was the Pope's third miracle?
He cured a ham.

❧

Did you hear about the Pope's plan to redecorate the Sistine Chapel?
. . . in knotty pine?

❧

You know why the Pope didn't want to accept the position?
It meant moving into an Italian neighborhood.

❧

What kind of meat does the Pope eat?
Nun.

❧

A rabbi, a priest, and a minister were having a discussion as to how they divided up the collection plate. The minister explained that he drew a circle on the ground, tossed the collection in the air, and that all the money that landed in the circle was for God and all that landed outside was for himself and the parish. The priest said that his system was similar: He just drew a straight line, tossed the money up, and that what landed on one side was for God and on the other for himself and the church. The rabbi admitted that his system worked along somewhat the same lines. "I just toss the plate up in the air," he explained, "and anything God can catch he can keep."

෴

Christ is on the cross, and Peter is down the hill comforting Mary Magdalene when he hears in a faint voice, "Peter . . . Peter . . ."

"I must go and help my Savior," he said and went up the hill, only to be beaten and kicked back down by the Roman centurions guarding the cross. But soon he hears, "Peter . . . Peter" in even fainter tones, and he cannot ignore the call. Peter limps up the hill, leans a ladder against the cross, and is halfway up when the centurions knock over the ladder, beat him brutally, and toss him back down the hill.

Again he hears, "Peter . . . Peter . . ." ever fainter, and he cannot sit idle. He staggers up the hill, drags himself up the ladder, and finally gets even with Christ's face. Just as the centurions are reaching for the ladder, Christ says, "Peter . . . Peter . . . I can see your house from here."

A little Catholic kid was praying as hard as he could. "God," he prayed, "I really want a car." Jumping up and dashing to the window, he saw that the driveway was empty.

"God," he prayed again, "I really *need* a car." Still no answer to his prayers. Suddenly the kid stood up, ran into his parents' bedroom, and grabbed the statuette of the Virgin Mary off the mantelpiece. He wrapped it up in ten layers of paper, using three rolls of tape and a spool of twine, then stuffed it inside a box at the very bottom of his closet.

"Okay, God," he said, getting down onto his knees again, "if you ever want to see your mother again . . ."

༄

Why does the Pope wear gym shorts?

He doesn't want to look down on the unemployed.

༄

Two nuns were taking a stroll through the park at dusk when two men jumped them, ripped off their habits, and proceeded to rape them.

Sister Gregory, bruised and battered, looked up at the sky and said softly, "Forgive him, Lord, for he knows not what he does."

Sister Theresa looked over at her and said, "Mine does."

What's black and red and has trouble getting through a revolving door?

A nun with a spear through her head.

∾

Two bishops were discussing the decline in morals in the modern world. "I didn't sleep with my wife before I was married," said one clergyman self-righteously. "Did you?"

"I don't know, said the other. "What was her maiden name?"

∾

Three nuns die and go to heaven, where they are warmly welcomed at the Pearly Gates by St. Peter. "Sisters," he says, "I want to thank you for all your good work on earth. Now there's just a brief formality before I can admit you to heaven: Each of you will have to answer one question." And, turning to the first nun, he asks, "Sister Michael, what is the Mystery of the Trinity?"

"That's the Father, Son, and the Holy Ghost," she replies. And the lights flash, the bells go off, and Sister Michael is swept into the Pearly Gates.

"Sister Benedicta," asks St. Peter gently, "what is the Mystery of the Virgin Birth?"

"That's the Immaculate Conception," she replied,

and she too is swept inside the gates with much flashing of lights and sounding of bells.

Sister Angelica is left alone, shaking a bit with nervousness. St. Peter turns to her and asks, "What, Sister Angelica, were the first words Eve said to Adam?"

Sister Angelica thought it over, beads of sweat starting to appear on her brow, and finally blurted, "Gee, Saint Peter, that's a hard one."

And the bells went off, the gates opened . . .

∾

Jesus was making his usual rounds in heaven when he noticed a wizened, white-haired old man sitting in a corner looking very disconsolate. The next week he was disturbed to come across him again, looking equally miserable, and a week later he stopped to talk to him.

"See here, old fellow," said Jesus kindly, "this is heaven. The sun is shining, you've got all you could want to eat, all the instruments you might want to play—you're supposed to be blissfully happy! What's wrong?"

"Well," said the old man, "you see, I was a carpenter on earth, and lost my only, dearly beloved son at an early age. And here in heaven I was hoping more than anything to find him."

Tears sprang to Jesus' eyes. "Father!" he cried.

The old man jumped to his feet, bursting into tears, and sobbed, "Pinocchio!"

Three Irish women were passing the time of day on the street corner, the street corner that just happened to be opposite the local whorehouse. And when the rabbi went in the door, there was a great clucking of tongues. Next to enter was the Episcopal minister. "Can you believe it?" said one woman to the rest. "The state of the clergy today is positively disgraceful."

Last to enter was Father Flanigan.

"Ah," said the women. "She must be very sick."

A drunk was staggering down the main street of the town. Somehow he managed to make it up the stairs to the cathedral and into the building, where he crashed from pew to pew, finally making his way to a side aisle and into a confessional.

A priest had been observing the man's sorry progress and, figuring the fellow was in need of some assistance, proceeded to enter his side of the confessional. But his attention was rewarded only by a lengthy silence. Finally he asked, "May I help you, my son?"

"I dunno," came the drunk's voice from behind the partition. "You got any paper on your side?"

Three young men presented themselves at the monastery as candidates for entering the monastic order. A stern-looking monk gave them a lecture about the privations of the monastic life, then showed them all into a small room, explaining that there was one preliminary test before they could be accepted as candidates. Ordering them to strip naked, he tied a little bell to each of their penises, then left the room. The next time the door opened, it was to admit a lovely young woman in a bikini, who exited to the tinkling of one of the bells.

"Oh, please, please, give me another trial run," pleaded the guilty party. But the next time the door opened, the lovely young woman was completely naked, the bell rang even more energetically.

"I'm sorry," explained the monk, "but you are clearly not suited for this life. I must ask you to leave."

Crushed, the young man bent over to pick up his clothes. And the other two bells went off.

❧

Three guys die and are transported to the Pearly Gates, where St. Peter greets them warmly, explaining that there's just one brief formality before they can be admitted to heaven. Each will have to answer one quick question. Turning to the first fellow, he asks, "What, please, is Easter?"

"That's an easy one. That's to celebrate when the Pilgrims landed. You buy a turkey and really stuff yourselves—"

"I'm sorry," interrupts St. Peter. "You're out." Turning to the second man, he asks, "What can you tell me about Easter?"

"No problem," he replies. "To commemorate the birth of Jesus, you go out shopping and get this tree and all these presents—"

"Forget it," says St. Peter, turning in disgust to the third man. "I don't suppose you'd know anything about Easter?"

"Certainly," he replies. "You see, Christ was crucified and he died, and they took the body down from the cross and wrapped it in a shroud and put it in a cave and rolled this big stone across the entrance—"

"Wait a minute, wait a minute," interrupts St. Peter excitedly, waving for the first two guys to come over. "We got someone here who knows his stuff."

"And after three days they roll the stone away," continues the third guy, "and if he sees his shadow there's going to be six more weeks of winter."

Famous Dead People

What did Grace Kelly have that Natalie Wood could've used?

A good stroke.

❧

Did you hear the new national anthem of Monaco?

"She'll Be Comin' 'Round the Mountain When She Comes . . ."

❧

Did you hear Prince Rainier finally got some good news?

The car is covered by insurance.

Did you know that Princess Grace was on the radio? And on the dashboard and on the steering wheel . . .

ᘗ

What would Princess Grace be doing if she were alive today?
Scratching at the inside of her coffin.

ᘗ

Did you hear about the new Vic Morrow movie?
Blade Runner II. It's being made in two parts.

ᘗ

One day in heaven John Lennon was sitting around looking pretty blue. Luckily Steve McQueen was on the next cloud over, and he came by and asked Lennon how come he was so down-in-the-mouth.

"Oh, I miss Yoko and Sean and my fans, I guess," said Lennon. "It's just not as much fun being dead as it was being alive."

"Well cheer up," said McQueen, "I'm having a party."

So Lennon was looking pretty cheerful when Bob Marley drifted by a few hours later. "What's happening, mon?" he asked. "Why you look so cheerful?"

"Steve McQueen's having a party and I'm invited," explained Lennon happily, only to have his face fall when Marley told him the party had been cancelled. "How come?" he asked dejectedly.

"Bobby Sands came early," explained Marley, "and he ate all the food."*

∽

How did they know Vic Morrow had dandruff?"
    They found his head and shoulders in the bushes.

∽

Who taught Grace Kelley to drive?
    Ted Kennedy.

∽

What kind of wood doesn't float?
    Natalie Wood.

∽

Why didn't Natalie shower on the boat?
    She preferred to wash up on shore.

* Please keep in mind the gruesome deaths of all of these people, Bobby Sands was an Irish hunger striker, remember?

What's blue and sings alone?
    Dan Ackroyd.

∾

What's the difference between a moose and Guy Lombardo's orchestra?
    With a moose, the horns are in front and the asshole's in the rear.

∾

Did you hear Grace Kelly and Patricia Neal were to have made a movie together?
    Called *Different Strokes.*

∾

Did you know Vic Morrow's been made an honorary member of the Rotary Club?

∾

You know what's next door to the Joan Crawford Daycare Center in Hollywood?
    The Grace Kelly Driving School. (Also the store where they sell Natalie Wood Water Wings and the William Holden Drinking Helmet.)

Dead Baby

What does it take to make a dead baby float?
One scoop of ice cream and one scoop of dead
baby.

∾

How did the dead baby cross the road?
Stapled to the chicken.

∾

What's the difference between unloading a truckload
of dead babies and a truckload of bowling balls?
You can use a pitchfork on the dead babies.

Why do they boil water when a baby's being born?
So that if it's born dead, they can make soup.

∽

How do you fit a thousand dead babies in a phone booth?
La Machine!

∽

How do you get them out?
With a straw!

∽

What's red and squirms in the corner?
A baby playing with a razor blade.

∽

What's blue and squirms in the corner?
A baby in a baggie.

∽

What's green and sits in the corner?
The same baby two weeks later.

Blanche Knott

What's red and hangs from the ceiling?
    A baby on a meathook.

⌒

Why do you put a baby in the blender feet first?
    So you can watch its expression.

⌒

What's the perfect gift for a dead baby?
    A dead puppy.

⌒

What's red and goes around and around?
    A baby in a garbage disposal.

⌒

What's red and bubbly and scratches at the window?
    A baby in a microwave.

Animals

A young man was delighted to finally be asked home to meet the parents of the young woman he'd been seeing for some time. He was quite nervous about the meeting, though, and by the time he arrived punctually at the doorstep he was in a state of gastric distress. The problem developed into one of acute flatulence, and halfway through the canapés the young man realized he couldn't hold it in one second longer without exploding. A tiny fart escaped.

"Spot!" called out the young woman's mother to the family dog, lying at the young man's feet.

Relieved at the dog's having been blamed, the young man let another, slightly larger one go.

"Spot!" she called out sharply.

"I've got it made," thought the fellow to himself. One more and I'll feel fine. So he let loose a really big one.

"*Spot!*" shrieked the mother. "Get over here before he shits on you!"

If a stork delivers white babies and a crow delivers black babies, what kind of bird delivers no babies?

A swallow.

⧬

What do you get when you cross a deer and a pickle?

A dildo.

⧬

This little kid is taking a walk with his father around the neighborhood and what should they come across in an empty lot but two dogs going at it furiously. "Daddy," asked the kid, tugging on his father's sleeve, "what are those dogs doing?"

"Well, Billy, said his father, "they're making puppies."

A week later Billy gets thirsty in the middle of the night and wanders into his parents' bedroom, catching them in the act. "Daddy," he asks plaintively, "what are you and Mommy doing?"

"Well, Billy," says his slightly red-faced father, "we're making babies."

"Daddy, Daddy," cries Billy, "roll her over—I'd rather have puppies."

What do you call a cow who's had an abortion?
  Decaffeinated.

❦

What do a walrus and Tupperware have in common?
  They both like a tight seal.

❦

What's the last thing that goes through a bug's mind before hitting the windshield at 80 mph?
  Its asshole.

❦

A man was surprised by the sight of a fellow walking down the sidewalk holding a three-legged pig on a leash. Unable to restrain his curiosity, he crossed the street and said to the guy, "That's quite a pig you have there."

"Let me tell you about this pig," said the guy. "This pig is the most amazing animal that ever lived. Why, one night my house caught on fire when my wife and I were out, and this pig carried my three children to safety and put out the fire before the firemen could get there."

"Wow!" said the first man. "But what about . . ."

"And that's not all," interrupted the guy. "My house was broken into when my wife and I were sound asleep, and this pig had the valuables back in place and the thief in a half Nelson before we got to the bottom of the stairs."

"That's pretty impressive," conceded his listener. "But how come . . ."

"And listen to this!" burst in the guy. "When I fell through some thin ice while skating, this pig dove in and pulled me out and safely to shore. This pig saved my life!"

"That's really great," said the first man, "but I have to know one thing. How come the pig only has three legs?"

"Hey listen," replied the proud owner, "a pig like this you can't eat all at once."

❧

What's brown and white, lives in the forest, and doesn't have a mother?

Bambi.

This hot and dusty cowboy rode in from the mesa, filthy and exhausted. He obviously had had nothing but his horse for company for a couple of weeks and was looking forward to a couple of cold beers in the saloon. Swinging off his horse and hitching it to the rail, the cowboy gave his horse an affectionate slap on the neck. Then he astonished an old cowhand lounging on the porch by moving around to the horse's hindquarters, lifting up its tail, and planting a demure kiss on its asshole.

"What'd you do *that* for?" asked the cowhand, completely repulsed.

"Chapped lips," said the cowboy, heading for the saloon doors.

"Wait a minute," said the old guy. "Whaddaya mean, chapped lips?"

"Keeps ya from lickin' 'em," explained the cowboy.

༜

Why don't bunnies make noise when they screw?

They have cotton balls.

༜

A guy returns from a long trip to Europe, having left his beloved cat in his brother's care. The minute he's cleared customs, he calls up his brother and inquires after his pet.

"Your cat's dead," replies his brother bluntly.

The guy is devastated. "You know how much that cat meant to me," he moaned into the phone. "Couldn't you at least have thought of a nicer way of breaking the news? Couldn't you have said, 'Well, you know, the cat got out of the house one day and climbed up on the roof, and the fire department couldn't get her down, and finally she died of exposure . . . or starvation . . . or something'? Why are you always so thoughtless?"

"Look, I'm sorry," said his brother. "I'll try to do better next time."

"Okay, let's put it behind us. How are you, anyway? How's Mom?"

His brother is silent a moment. "Uh," he stammers, "uh . . . Mom's on the roof."

❧

Why does Miss Piggy douche with vinegar and honey?
Kermit likes sweet-and-sour pork.

❧

This guy walks into a psychiatrist's office with a duck on his head. "May I help you?" politely inquires the psychiatrist.

"Yeah," says the duck. "Get this guy off my ass."

What's the difference between a rooster and a whore?

A rooster says cock-a-doodle-doo; a whore says, "Any cock'll do."

How about the difference between a rooster and a lawyer?

A rooster clucks defiance . . .

❧

Do you know why the British ships came back from the Falkland Islands full of sheep?

War brides.

❧

This big black guy comes into a bar in the deep South with an alligator on a leash. "You serve martinis?" he asks the bartender, who's eyeing him suspiciously.

"Yes, we do."

"You serve niggers?"

"Yes, we do."

"I'll have a martini for myself," says the guy, "and a nigger for my alligator."

❧

What does an elephant use for a tampon?

A sheep.

What do elephants use for condoms?
  Goodyear blimps.

❧

Why did the rooster cross the basketball court?
  He heard the ref was blowing fouls.

❧

Why does an elephant have four feet?
  Eight inches isn't enough.

❧

Where's an elephant's sex organ?
  In his feet. If he steps on you, you're fucked.

❧

What do you do when you come across an elephant?
  Wipe it off.

❧

  Did you hear about the alligators in Florida sporting little Jews on their T-shirts?

How about the flamingos in Florida with pink cement Italians on their lawns?

༄

What do you get when you cross a Pole and a monkey?

Nothing. A monkey's too smart to fuck a Pole.

༄

Did you hear about James Watts' appearance on Julia Child's cooking class?

Giving lessons in how to carve a California condor ...

༄

How can you tell if you're overweight?

If you step on your dog's tail and it dies.

༄

Why do crabs have circles under their eyes?

From sleeping in snatches.

༄

Bumper sticker: NUKE THE WHALES!

A doctor, a lawyer, and an architect were arguing about who had the smartest dog. They decided to settle the issue by getting all the dogs together and seeing whose could perform the most impressive feat.

"Okay, Rover," said the architect, and Rover trotted over to a table and in ten minutes had constructed a full-scale model of Chartres out of toothpicks. Pretty impressive, everyone agreed, and the architect gave Rover a cookie.

"Hit it, Spot," said the doctor, and Spot lost no time in performing an emergency cesarian section on a cow, with mom and baby coming through the operation in fine shape. Not bad, conceded the other two, and Spot got a cookie from the doctor.

"Go, Fella," ordered the lawyer. So Fella fucked the other two dogs, took their cookies, and went out to lunch.

An elephant was walking along the jungle path when he got a thorn in his foot. He was unable to extract it and gave up all hope until an ant came along the same path. "Ant," said the elephant, "will you get this thorn out of my foot?"

"If I get to do what I want to do," piped the ant.

And what was that? inquired the elephant.

"I want to fuck you in the ass," the ant replied.

Well, the elephant's foot was hurting pretty badly by then, so he told the ant he had a deal (and besides, how bad could it be?). After a few minutes the ant succeeded in working the thorn free. "Are you ready now, elephant?" he piped. Being an honorable elephant, he conceded he was as ready as he was ever going to be and lay still while the ant made his laborious way around to his ass, heaved his tail out of the way, and began to fuck him in the ass.

A monkey high in a tree witnessed the entire transaction. Unable to contain his hysteria at the sight of the ant pumping away at the elephant's rear, he began to heave coconuts down at the beast. He managed to hit the elephant square on the head, eliciting a pained, "Ouch!"

"Take it all, bitch!" squealed the ant.

❧

What can you do with a dog with no legs?

Take it for a drag .

❧

A guy comes into a bar and the first thing he sees in the middle of the room is an enormous alligator. He spins around and is hustling out the door when the bartender says, "Hey, hold it! Come on back in; this alligator's tame. Look, I'll show you."

He comes out from behind the bar, tells the alligator to open its mouth, unzips his pants and whips it out, and stands there with his pecker in the alligator's mouth for a full fifteen minutes.

"Pretty amazing, huh?" he says, turning around and zipping himself up. "You wanna give it a try?"

"Gee, I don't think so," says the first man. "I don't think I could keep my mouth open for fifteen minutes."

❦

An old lady is rocking away the last of her days on her front porch, reflecting on her long life, when all of a sudden a fairy godmother appears in front of her in a beautiful, shining blue gown and tells her she can have any three wishes she wants.

"Well," says the little old lady, "I guess I'd like to be really rich."

And—poof!—her rocking chair turns into solid gold.

"And, gee, I guess I wouldn't mind being changed into a lovely young princess."

And—poof!—she's metamorphosed into a dazzling young woman.

"You get a third wish," reminds the fairy godmother gently, and just then the old lady's cat walks across the porch in front of them.

"Can you change him into a handsome prince?" she asks, and—poof!—there before her stands a young man more handsome than her wildest imaginings.

With a smile that makes her knees weak, he saunters across the porch and whispers in her ear, "Aren't you sorry you had me neutered?"

Did you hear about the Polish fox that caught its paw in a trap?

It gnawed off three feet before it got free.

⟡

What does an elephant use for a vibrator?

An epileptic.

⟡

What do you do with an elephant with three balls?

Walk him and pitch to the rhino.

⟡

A guy comes into the bar with a frog and sets it down next to the prettiest girl there. "This is a very special frog," he informs her. "His name is Charlie."

"What's so special about this frog?" she asks. He's reluctant to tell her, but when pressed, explains that, "This frog can eat pussy."

The girl slaps him, knocking him off his chair, and accuses him of telling her a filthy lie. But no, he assures her, it's completely true. And after much discussion, she agrees to come back to his apartment to see the frog in action. She positions herself appropriately, the guy carefully takes out the frog, and says, "Okay, Charlie, do your stuff!"

The frog is immobile, despite his owner's exhortations, and the girl starts to snicker.

"Okay, Charlie," says the guy, moving the frog out of the way, "I'm only going to show you one more time."

~

What's the difference between meat and fish?
If you beat your fish, it dies.

~

How do you get virgin wool?
From ugly sheep.

~

Why do ducks have webbed feet?
To stamp out forest fires.
Why do elephants have big, flat feet?
To stamp out flaming ducks.

~

What did one Muppet say to the other?
"I can't talk now—I've got a frog in my throat.

What's red and green and goes up and down and up and down?

A frog in a blender.

∽

What do you get when you cross a Pole and a gorilla?

A retarded gorilla.

∽

A man comes into a tavern and puts his legless dog down on the bar. The bartender comes up to ask him for his order and says, by the way of friendly conversation, "What's your dog's name?"

"He doesn't have a name," says the man.

The bartender fixes a second round and, in the process, can't resist asking, "C'mon, what's the dog's name?"

"I told you he doesn't have one."

Over the third round the bartender leans conspiratorially over the bar and says, "I just can't believe you. Every dog has a name."

"Not this one," says the man. "What's the good of it? He can't come when I call."

What do you call a masturbating bull?
 Beef Stroganoff.

❧

 This blind fellow walked into Macy's with his seeing-eye dog and headed straight for the men's department. Surrounded by pajamas and neckties, he proceeded to come to a stop, pick up his German Shepherd by the hind legs, and swing the dog around and around in a circle.
 A startled clerk ran over to him, saying loudly, "Sir . . . may I help you with anything?"
 "No thanks," said the blind man, "just looking."

❧

What's invisible and smells like rabbit?
 Bunny farts.

❧

 A flea had oiled up his little flea legs and his little flea arms, had spread out his blanket, and was proceeding to soak up the Miami sun when who should stumble by on the beach but an old flea friend of his.
 "Oscar, what happened to you?" asked the flea, because Oscar looked pretty terrible, wrapped up in

a blanket, his nose running, his eyes red, and his teeth chattering.

"I got a ride down here in some guy's mustache . . . and he came down by motorcycle. I nearly froze my nuts off," wheezed Oscar.

"Let me give you a tip, old pal," said the first flea, spreading some more suntan oil on his shoulders. "You go to the stewardesses' lounge at the airport, see, and you get up on a toilet seat, and when an Air Florida stew comes in to take a leak, you hop on for a nice, warm ride. Got it?"

So you can imagine the flea's surprise when, a month or so later, while stretched out all warm and comfortable on the beach, whom should he see but Oscar—looking more chilled and miserable than before.

"Listen," said Oscar before the other flea could say a word, "I did everything you said. I made it to the stewardesses' lounge and waited till a really cute one came in, made a perfect landing, and got so warm and cozy that I dozed right off."

"And so?" asked the flea.

"And so the next thing I know I'm on some guy's mustache . . ."

❧

How can you tell when an elephant's got her period?
    There's a nickel on the bedstand, and your mattress is missing.

Herpes

What's the difference between mono and herpes?
You get mono when you snatch a kiss.

∼

Did you hear about the Polish hooker with herpes?
She charged extra for multiple organisms.

∼

What's the fourth biggest lie?
It's only a cold sore.

Totally Tasteless

Did you hear about the gay guy who was so hip he got Herpes III?

～

Did you hear about the cure for herpes?
    Extra-Strength Tylenol.

～

What do you call herpes above *and* below the waist?
    Herpes duplex.

～

What do you get when you fuck a midget?
    Twerpies.
When you fuck a bird?
    Chirpies.
And when you fuck ice cream?
    Slurpies.

～

What's the difference between love and herpes?
    Herpes is forever.

Lepers

*D*id *you hear about the leper who made his living*
as a gigolo?

He was doing great until business fell off.

∽

Why was time-out called in the leper hockey game?

There was a face-off in the corner.

∽

How can you tell when a valentine is from a leper?

The tongue's in the envelope.

How could you tell when the poker game between lepers was over?
    Someone threw his hand in.

∾

Why did the brothel in the leper colony close down?
    The tips weren't worth it.

∾

What did the leper say to the prostitute?
    Keep the tip.

∾

What's a leper in the bathtub?
    Stew.

∾

Know anyone who wants to do charity work in India?
    They need people to sort unclaimed feet in the leper colony.

Miscellaneous

A stuck-up fellow comes into a bar and proclaims himself the finest wine connoisseur in the city. He's so good, in fact, that he can identify the vintage and vineyard of any wine they carry, just from a sip.

Skeptical, the barman puts down a glass of white in front of him. "Pinot Grigio from Abruzzi," he proclaims. "1979 was a very poor year; please offer me something better the next time." Next is a rich glass of red. "Mouton Lafitte Rothschild, 1956. From the first row of vines on the westernmost hill. Quite delicious." The man goes on to correctly identify Californian reds, Spanish rosés, and sweet German whites, until the bartender is sick to death of him. Turning aside, he discreetly pees in a glass, chills it, and sets it before the connoisseur.

"Why that's *piss*," he splutters, spitting it on the floor.

"Yeah," says the bartender, "but whose?"

There was a wealthy old gentleman who desired the services of a prostitute, so he arranged with a call-girl to send over their $1000, top-of-the-line girl. She got all dolled up, rode over to his fancy apartment building, and was escorted up to his penthouse, where the door was opened by the elderly millionaire himself. "And what can I do for you tonight, sir?" she asked in her throatiest voice, dropping her fur coat to reveal a slinky lamé dress.

"Hot tub," he said.

So they went into his luxuriously appointed bathroom where she settled him into the tub. "And now, sir?" she asked.

"Waves," he said.

So she perched herself on the edge of the tub and proceeded to kick her feet vigorously to make waves. "And *next*, sir?"

"Thunder."

Obligingly banging her hand against the side of the tub, she felt it necessary to remind him that he was paying $1000 for her special services, and surely there was some sort of special service she could perform for him.

"Yes," he said, "lightning."

Kicking her feet in the water, banging on the side of the tub with one hand, and flicking the light switch on and off with the other, she felt obliged to give it one more shot. "Sir, you know I am a hooker . . . Uh, sexual matters are my specialty . . . Isn't there something along those lines you'd be interested in?"

"In *this* weather?" he said, looking up at her. "Are you crazy?"

Three old guys are sitting around in the park, discussing whose memory goes back the farthest. Says Larry, "I remember being taken to the church, all dressed up in this scratchy white stuff, and having people standing around and someone splashing water on me."

"Aww, that's nothing," says Irv. "I can remember this nice, dark room, and then being squeezed something terrible, and coming out into this big bright room and being spanked—it was awful."

"I got you two beat by a mile," says Fred. "I remember going to a picnic with my father and coming back with my mother."

❧

What's blue and comes in Brownies?
    Cub Scouts.

❧

What's gray and comes in quarts?
    Elephants.

❧

Why do Valley Girls wear two diaphragms?
    Fer shurr, fer shurr.

The Israelites were all waiting anxiously at the foot of the mountain, knowing that Moses had had a tough day negotiating with God over the Commandments. Finally a tired Moses came into sight. "I've got some good news and some bad news, folks," he said. "The good news is that I got Him down to ten. The bad news is that adultery's still in."

∽

You know why sex is like a bridge game?
    You don't need a partner if you have a good hand.

∽

What's the definition of mixed emotions?
    When you see your mother-in-law backing off a cliff in your brand new Mercedes.

∽

Did you hear that Air Florida now serves Key Largo, Key West . . . and Key Bridge?
    That they've got two new classes besides smoking and nonsmoking . . . swimming and nonswimming?
    That they have free drinks on all flights . . . they just have to stop and pick up the ice.

Which of the following words is out of place: *wife, dog, meat, blow job?*

Blow job. You can beat your wife, you can beat your dog, and you can beat your meat, but nothing beats a blow job.

∿

What do cowboy hats and hemorrhoids have in common?

Sooner or later every asshole has one.

∿

Two little kids, aged six and eight, decide it's time to learn how to swear. So the eight-year-old says to the six-year-old, "Okay, you say 'ass' and I'll say 'hell.'"

All excited about their plan, they troop downstairs, where their mother asks them what they'd like for breakfast. "Aw, hell," says the eight-year-old, "gimme some Cheerios." mother backhands him off the stool, sending him bawling out of the room, and turns to the younger brother. "What'll you have?"

"I dunno," quavers the six-year-old, "but you can bet your ass it ain't gonna be Cheerios."

How do you get twenty Argentines into a phone booth?

Tell 'em they own it.

❧

What's the difference between erotic and kinky?

Erotic is when you use a feather; kinky is when you use the whole chicken.

❧

Why did Begin besiege Beirut?

To impress Jodie Foster.

❧

The newlywed couple is ushered into the doctor's office. The husband is clearly embarrassed by the circumstances, but makes it clear that the visit is his idea. "You see, doctor," he confides, "my wife, she eats like a horse."

"That's absolutely nothing to be concerned about," says the doctor reassuringly. "Many young women have surprisingly hearty appetites."

"Oh I know, doctor," says the young man. "But my wife spends all day on all fours in the barn, and all she'll eat is barley, oats, and hay."

"Hmmm," says the doctor, sitting and thinking

quietly for a few minutes. Then he turns and begins scribbling on a piece of paper.

"Can you cure her, doctor?" asks the new husband anxiously. "Is that some sort of prescription?"

"No, no, no," says the doctor. "It's a permit so she can shit in the streets."

༄

A lovelorn young man wrote to an advice columnist as follows:

Dear Abby,
   I just met the most terrific girl and we get along fabulously. I think she's the one for me. There's just one problem: I can't remember from our first date if she told me she had T.B. or V.D. What should I do?

—Confused

Abby replies:

Dear Confused,
   If she coughs, fuck her.

༄

First guy: "Know how to keep an asshole in suspense?"
Second guy: "No, how?"
First guy: "I'll tell you later."

Why does Dolly Parton have such a small waist?
    Nothing grows in the shade.

❧

How can you tell Dolly Parton's kids in the playground?
    Stretch marks on their lips.

❧

Did you hear about the eighty-year-old man who streaked the flower show?
    He won first prize for his dried arrangement.

❧

How do you get a Kleenex to dance?
    Blow a little boogie into it.

❧

Joe: "How many birds in a flock?"
Sam: "I dunno."
Joe: "How many bees in a hive?"
Sam: "I dunno."
Joe: "How many lives does a cat have?"
Sam: "Nine."

Joe: "Well how come if you don't know shit about the birds and the bees, you know so much about pussy?"

∽

What's the worst thing about being an egg?
> You only get laid once; you only get eaten once; it takes you ten minutes to get hard and three minutes to get soft; you come in a box with eleven other guys; and only your mother sits on your face.

∽

What's the definition of a real buddy?
> Someone who'll go downtown and get two blow jobs, and come back and give you one.

∽

Two guys are walking across the street when they run into a mutual friend, and they comment on how prosperous-looking he is. It turns out he has every reason to be: he's got an eighty-foot yacht, a beautiful wife, a private jet plane, and a million dollars in the bank.

You can imagine their surprise when they run into him two weeks later, dressed in rags and shuffling along dejectedly. They press the sad story out of him. Apparently, he loaned the yacht to a friend who ran it aground and wrecked it, and he had no insurance.

"So?" say the two guys. "It's only a boat."

"Yes, but I didn't have any insurance on the jet either, and it was destroyed in a fire at the airstrip."

"Hey, take heart," say his friends, "at least you've still got your lovely wife and your bank balance."

"Not so fast, fellas," says the poor guy. "My wife ditched me for another guy and her lawyer took me for every cent I had. I'll tell you, if I've learned one thing from all of this, here's what it is: If it flies, floats, or fucks, lease it."

∾

What's the ultimate rejection?

Your hand falls asleep while you're masturbating.

∾

Did you hear about the latest over-the-counter scare?

Someone slipped Krazy Glue into Preparation H.

∾

This really conceited guy is fucking this really conceited girl.

Says she, "Aren't I tight?"

Says he, "No, just full."

Sam Lefkovitz is having an intimate party to celebrate his thirty immensely profitable years in the construction business. "You know," he laments to his friends, "over the years I have constructed dozens of enormous projects in and around this city, but am I known as Sam the Builder? No.

"And over the years I have contributed literally millions of dollars to charitable causes of one sort or another, but am I called Sam the Philanthropist? No, sir.

"But suck *one* little cock . . ."

ᘐ

What's organic dental floss?
Pubic hair.

ᘐ

Queen Elizabeth and Lady Di are out for a drive in the royal car on a Sunday afternoon, and they slow down when they see a man by the roadside signaling for help. But no sooner has the car come to a stop than he springs to the door, pulls out a gun, and orders them both out of the car. "Queen Elizabeth," he snarls, "hand over that snazzy diamond tiara you're always wearing."

"I'm terribly sorry, my good man," says the queen, "but I'm afraid I don't wear it on Sundays."

"Aw, hell," says the guy. "Well listen, Di, hand over

that fancy engagement ring I keep seeing in all the pictures."

"I'm terribly sorry," says Lady Di sweetly, "but I'm afraid I didn't put it on this morning. It must still be on my night table."

"Aw, shit," growls the guy. "I guess I'll just grab the car." So off he drives at the wheel of the Bentley, leaving the two women walking down the road in the direction of London. After a few minutes have passed, Lady Di asks the queen, "Pardon my curiosity, Your Highness, but I'm quite sure you had that tiara on this morning. Didn't you?"

"Indeed I did," confesses the queen, blushing slightly and pointing. "I hid it . . . down there. And you, Diana, weren't you wearing your ring?"

Yes she had been, says Diana, turning beet red, and she had resorted to the same hiding place.

They walk a few more steps in companionable silence when Queen Elizabeth lets out a little sigh. "I do wish Princess Margaret had been with us," she says. "We could have saved the Bentley."

◦∿◦

How do you fit five comedians in a Volkswagen?
    Two in the front seat, two in the back, and Richard Pryor in the ashtray.

◦∿◦

What's white and flies across the ocean?
    Lord Mountbatten's tennis shoes.

A doctor was walking down the hospital corridor and stopped to speak to the head nurse.

"Oh doctor," she said, "you've got your thermometer stuck behind your ear."

"Shit!" cried the doctor. "Some asshole has my pen!"

⌒

Have you ever smelled mothballs?

No! How do you get their legs apart?

⌒

Imagine the President's dismay when he woke up one winter morning in the White House to see outside his window, written in pee in the fresh snow, "The President sucks." Furious, he summoned the Secret Service, the police, and the FBI, and told them they had better come up with the culprit—fast.

That afternoon a hapless officer arrived in the Oval Office to give the President the results of their investigation. "We have definitely established that it's the Vice-President's urine," he said, "but I'm afraid it's the First Lady's handwriting."

⌒

What's the difference between a rock-and-roller and a pig?

A pig won't stay up all night to fuck a rock-and-roller.

What are the five biggest lies?
"The check is in the mail."
"I won't come in your mouth."
"Some of my best friends are Jewish."
"Black is beautiful."
"I'm from your government, and I'm here to help you."

～

How many punk rockers does it take to change a light bulb?
Two. One to change the bulb, and the other to kick the chair out from under him.

～

How many rednecks does it take to eat a 'possum?
Three. One to eat the 'possum, and two to watch for cars.

～

What's wrinkled and smells like Ginger?
Fred Astaire's face.

Two cannibals are having dinner together. The guest says to his host, "Your wife sure makes good soup."

"Yeah, but I'm going to miss her," his friend replies.

～

Harry and Rachel are celebrating their fiftieth wedding anniversary at the Fontainebleau and it's a hell of a party: champagne, caviar, toasts by all of their best friends who've assembled for the occasion. Finally, tired and happy, the couple retires to their luxurious suite.

"Rachel," says Harry, "you know, this would be the perfect evening if only . . ."

"Oh, Harry," sighs Rachel, "I thought you got over that years ago. You know I don't like it."

"But, Rachel, it's such a special night. Just this once . . ."

"Harry, you know how I feel about this sort of thing."

"I know, I know," pleads Harry, "but you know how much it'll mean to me."

So Rachel finally goes down on him. Just as she's finishing up, the phone rings.

Harry gets up on one elbow and says, "Answer the phone, cocksucker."

Why did the Dairy Queen get pregnant?
    Because the Burger King forgot to wrap his whopper.
Why *didn't* the Dairy Queen get pregnant?
    Because she went out with Mr. Softee.

~

Why is the Urban Cowboy's mustache all brown and scuzzy?
    He's lookin' for love in all the wrong places.

~

A guy was sitting have a few at the local pub when he observed a very lovely young woman sitting only a few chairs down. He moved over and proceeded to engage her in general conversation, finally screwing up his courage to ask her out to a movie.
    She hauled off and slugged him so hard he landed on his ass on the floor. "Gee," he said, picking himself up, "I guess a blow job is out of the question, huh?"

~

How can you tell the head nurse?
    By the dirt on her knees.

What do you call nuts on a wall?
    Walnuts.
What do you call nuts on a chest?
    Chestnuts.
What do you call nuts on a chin?
    A blow job.

∾

Why does Dr. Pepper come in a bottle?
    Because his wife died.

∾

What did Raggedy Anne say to Pinocchio as she was sitting on his face?
    "Tell the truth! Tell a lie! Tell the truth! Tell a lie!"

∾

A man was having a few in the local bar when he noticed a sailor sitting at the other end of the bar. The sailor had a completely normal physique except for one anomaly: his head was tiny, about the size of an orange.

The man stared at the sailor in puzzlement, and after a few more drinks screwed up his courage to go over and ask the sailor how his condition had come about.

The sailor took the question in good humor, and explained that some time ago he had been shipwrecked. "I came to," he explained, "on this beautiful little beach, and heard this sad little whimpering sound behind some rocks on the shore. Investigating, I saw that it was this gorgeous mermaid who had been stranded on the rocks, so I carried her back to the water's edge. And she was so grateful that she promised to grant me any three wishes. Well, as you can imagine, my first wish was that I get off that god-forsaken island in one piece.

" 'I'll grant you that one after you've had the first two,' she said.

"So next I told her I'd like to be rich beyond dreams. And—whammo—there on the beach appeared a chest full of gold and jewels. And then, being a normal sort of guy—and she was cute, believe me—I asked if we could make love.

" 'Look at me,' said the mermaid. It's easy to see I'm not built for that sort of thing.'

"So I says to her, 'Okay, how about a little head!' "

❧

What's the ultimate in courage?
Two cannibals having oral sex.

For decades two heroic bronze statues, one male and one female, faced each other in a city park, until one day an angel came down from heaven. "You've been such exemplary statues," he announced to them, "that I'm going to give you a special gift. I'm going to bring you both to life for thirty minutes, in which you can do anything you want to." And with a clap of his hand, the angel brought the statues to life.

The two approached each other a bit shyly but soon dashed for the bushes, from which shortly emerged a good deal of giggling, laughter, and shaking of branches. Fifteen minutes later the two statues emerged from the bushes, wide grins on their faces.

"You still have fifteen more minutes," said the angel, winking conspiratorially.

Grinning even more widely, the female statue turned to the male statue and said, "Great! Only this time you hold the pigeon down, and *I'll* shit on its head."

&

What's the black stuff between an elephant's toes?
   Slow natives.

&

The boss came in and asked the new secretary, "Ellen, do you know the difference between a Caesar Salad and a blow job?"

"No," she replied.

"Great! Let's have lunch."

A woman came to the supermarket, went over to the butcher counter, and announced her desire to buy a Long Island duck. The butcher, a recent employee, obligingly went into the back room and came out with a fine-looking duck.

The woman stuck her finger up the duck's ass and announced, "I'm sorry, this won't do. This is a Maine duck."

The butcher raised his eyebrows, but soon returned with another duck.

"No," pronounced the woman, her finger up the second duck's ass, "this duck is from Minnesota."

Barely restraining himself, the butcher fetched a third duck.

"Now this," said the woman, smiling after performing the same inspection, "this is a Long Island duck. Thank you so much." She was about to leave when she turned back to the counter and asked, "Say, you're new here, aren't you? Where are you from?

The butcher pulled down his pants, turned around, and said, "You tell me, lady."

∽

An aged couple showed up in their lawyer's office bright and early one morning and announced that they wanted a divorce.

"Gee," said the lawyer, "and at your age and after fifty years of married life. What brought about this decision now?"

"Well you see," explained the couple, "we wanted to wait until the children were dead."

A young guy had gone to his doctor for a routine checkup, and when he came in for the results, the doctor said gravely, "Jerry, I think you'd better sit down. I've got some good news and some bad news."

"Okay, Doc," said Jerry. "Give me the bad news first."

"Well," said the doctor, "you've got cancer. It's spreading at an unbelievably rapid rate, it's totally inoperable, and you've got about three weeks to live."

"Jesus," said Jerry, wiping a bead of sweat off his brow. "What's the *good* news?"

"You know that really cute receptionist out in the front office?"

"You bet!" said Jerry.

"The one with the big tits and the cute little ass?"

"Right!"

"And the long blond hair?"

"Yeah, yeah," said Jerry impatiently.

"Well," said the doctor, leaning forward with a smile, "I'm fucking her!"

Too Tasteless
To Be Included
in This Book

*W*hat do you have when you've got *10,000 blacks*
at the bottom of the ocean?
A good start.

∾

Why don't their mothers let little black kids play in
the sandbox?
Because the cats bury them.

∾

You know how fancy mail-order catalogs offer
those ridiculously expensive, exclusive items for sale?
In a recent one there was a full-page spread for a
$25,000 pair of boots made of human skin.
In fine print, at the bottom, it said, "In black, $7.50."

How do you baby-sit for a black kid?
     Wet its lips and stick it to the wall.
How do you get it unstuck?
     Teach it to say "motherfucker."

∽

What does a JAP do with her asshole in the morning?
     Sends him out to work.

∽

How do you stop five blacks from raping a white girl?
     Throw 'em a basketball.

∽

Did you hear about Ronald Reagan's new Kentucky Fried Chicken outlet?
     It only serves right wings and assholes.

∽

What do you do with a dead black?
     Carve him out and use him for a wet suit.

What's the difference between a mother-in-law and a bucket of shit?
  The bucket.

∿

What's yellow on the outside, black on the inside, and goes screaming over a cliff?
  A school bus full of black kids.

∿

What's the difference between a JAP and a toilet?
  A toilet doesn't follow you around for months after you use it.

∿

Why do women have legs?
  So they don't leave tracks like snails.

∿

How do you save a drowning Puerto Rican?
  You say you don't know? Good.

How do you get a Polish girl pregnant?
　　Come in her shoe and let the flies do the rest.

～

What's the difference between a slave and a tire?
　　A tire doesn't sing when you put the chains on.

～

What music did they play at Anwar Sadat's funeral?
　　I Love a Parade.

～

　　Two aged child molesters are sitting on a park bench, reminiscing about sexual adventures of their pasts. "Ah," sighs one, "I remember when I had an eight-year-old with the body of a four-year-old . . ."

～

How many blacks does it take to tar a roof?
　　A dozen, if you slice 'em thin enough.

An unfortunate fellow was locked up in the state penitentiary doing five to ten for armed robbery. And all he could think of the whole time he was locked up was eating pussy.

The day finally came for his release. He walked out of the prison with the new suit and the ten dollars the officials had given him, and made a beeline for the whorehouse in the nearest town. Slamming down his ten-dollar bill on the front desk, he said, "I wanna eat some pussy!"

"Where've you been," said the greasy fellow behind the desk. "Ten dollars these days don't buy more than a close look."

"Listen, buddy," said the ex-con, pulling him out of his chair by his shirt collar, "I wanna eat some pussy, and I want it *now*."

"Okay, okay," gasped the proprietor, "I'll see what I can do." So the ex-con followed him through to the very back of the whorehouse, through some stained, tattered red curtains, and into a grimy little room where a bedraggled-looking whore lay spreadeagled on a filthy bed. "She's yours for the ten dollars," said the proprietor, and the fellow went at it.

After a little while, he came across a piece of egg. "That's funny," he thought to himself, "I don't think I had eggs for breakfast." But he spat it out and kept eating away. Next he found a piece of chipped beef wedged between his front teeth. "I'm sure I haven't eaten chipped beef this week," he thought, but he kept on. Then he came across the corn.

"I *know* I haven't eaten any corn lately," he said, sitting up. "I think I'm going to be sick."

"Ya know," said the whore, "that's what the last guy said."

⌒

Why do blacks smell?
    So that blind people can hate them too.

⌒

A trucker was carrying a load of bowling balls down the thruway when to his horror, the tailgate unfastened and hundreds of them went rolling across the road. He brought the big truck to a stop as fast as he could and ran back to the scene of the accident —only to see, to his astonishment, dozens of Poles already busy smashing the bowling balls with axes and sledgehammers and any other blunt instruments on hand.

"What the hell are you doing?" he asked.

"You gotta get these nigger eggs before they hatch," they explained.

⌒

What's the American dream?
    A million blacks swimming back to Africa with a Jew under each arm.

What's the definition of bad acne?
    Waking up in the park with a blind man reading your face.

⁓

Why does Hellen Keller wear skin tight pants?
    So that people can read her lips.

A NOTE ABOUT THE AUTHOR

Blanche Knott is the author's real name. However, her family lives pseudonymously in Washington D.C. where she is no longer welcome. She currently lives in New York City. Her favorite color is brown.

A NOTE ABOUT THE TYPE

The text of this book was set on the Linotype in Janson, a recutting made direct from the type cast from matrices long thought to have been made by Anton Janson, a Dutchman who was a practicing type-founder in Leipzig during the years 1668–1687. However, it has been conclusively demonstrated that these types are actually the work of Nicholas Kis (1650–1702), a Hungarian who learned his trade most probably from the master Dutch type-founder Dirk Voskens.

The type is an excellent example of the influential and sturdy Dutch types that prevailed in England prior to the development by William Caslon (1692–1766) of his own incomparable designs, which he evolved from these Dutch faces. The Dutch in their turn had been influenced by Claude Garamond (1510–1561) in France. The general tone of the Janson, however, is darker than Garamond and has a sturdiness and substance quite different from its predecessors.

Composed by MARYLAND LINOTYPE COMPOSITION COMPANY, INC., Baltimore, Maryland. Printed and bound by R.R. DONNELLEY & SONS CO., Harrisonburg, Virginia. Typography and binding design by IRIS BASS.